THERE ARE PROBLEMS IN THE
BODY OF CHRST
AND
THIS IS

WHAT

OUGHT

TO

BE

By

Doug Ball

OTHER CHRISTAIN BOOKS

BY

PASTOR DOUG

PUZZING THEOLOGY

A modern parable
of Christian growth.

A must for the deep thinker.

THE FISHY PROPHET

A Bible study
on the book of Jonah.
With an emphasis on the Christian Call.

Available in paperback or ebook

@

www.amazon.com/author/dougball

This book is dedicated to my
Lord and Savior
who gave His life
that thru His Grace
I might live a
wild and crazy life
imitating Him
for His sake.

I am but a sinner saved by Grace.
I take little seriously except
the
Kingdom of God.

and
Pastor Larry Hamblin
The Right Reverend Tom White
My right hand man in service David Dehner
Steve Coombe

and
my editor, confidant, and wife
Patti

FOR YOUR BENEFIT, PLEASE READ: This book has a lot of white space. All for one reason, YOU. You can read a book and do nothing other than say, "I have read another book on saving the church." OR, you can read, take notes, jot in the margins, and even doodle while you're thinking with white space like this. Also, you can contact me if you think I'm way off base, have a question, a suggestion, or even just wanna chat.

Email – **pastordougbooks@gmail.com**

Phone – 928 245 1667 leave a message if I don't answer and I will get back soonest

Mail – P O Box 1128

St. Johns, AZ 85936

It just doesn't get much better than that.

SEE THE END OF THIS BOOK FOR OTHER BOOKS BY THIS AUTHOR AND THE SAME CONTACT INFORMATION AGAIN.

Rise up and Praise the Lord
with your life.
HE
gave His.

Introduction

The collective Church in the USA is in trouble, many of the same troubles that plague the church in Europe. The numbers are going down and the Western church has lost its significance. If 70-80% of the people in the USA consider themselves Christian, why don't they have significance? Why aren't they a major voting block to be catered to in the political campaigns? Why is it okay to be anything else, but not a Christian? Why can anyone that wants to slander, backbite, and smear the Church with impunity?

Perhaps it's because the Church in the West is not being THE CHURCH.

The Church is still based on Faith in Jesus Christ, nothing more and nothing less. Nothing has changed in the purpose statement and values of THE CHURCH.

But, there is a problem with the Church in the West today and it is serious. Numbers of members in the Churches are not keeping up with population increase, in fact numbers are dropping as more and more people just plain drop out after finding nothing in the Church to cling to, not even faith.

The modern church has tried some serious innovations to market itself. It has:

> Put on a bigger show

> Gone to one dynamic preacher covering multiple sites using video

> Spent massive amounts of money advertising

> Given door prizes

> Given gas cards

> Thrown massive parties

> Spent big bucks attracting kids

> Demanded more education for its Pastors

> Spent extra-large dollars for sound and video systems

> Built massive campuses with all kinds of bells and whistles to attract people

> Used every medium imaginable

> Developed a bazillion Bible translations

> Turned to an "Easy Believeism" instead of a message of "Grace and Truth."

> Allowed wacko frauds and errant messages to go unchallenged

> Conformed to the world

- ➢ Allowed without challenge errant lifestyles and leadership
- ➢ Failed to challenge sin in its midst
- ➢ Fished in the same old ponds and not reached out to the new sources

Yes, there are faithful followers and congregations that are walking in the Word.

Ed Stetzer, a church health guru, has completed yet another poll and stated the outcomes of that poll. The term Christian will be used less and less, and will have modifiers to clarify.

- ➢ Non-Christian – 25% of population
- ➢ Cultural Christian – I am born in the USA, I am a Christian. 25%
- ➢ Congregational Christian – I go to church. 25%
- ➢ Convictional Christian – Born again, changed, living it. 25%

He further states that the Cultural and Congregational Christians will eventually become non-Christians, leaving the Convictional Christians as a robust, healthy Church with greater impact in communities because the distractive and destructive forces will be gone.

Even with these numbers, Christians in the last two categories should provide for a reasonably influential group in political circles and communities. With just the Convictional Christians, a 25% voting block is not to be sneezed at and yet the politicians make little effort to attract them. If that related to a 25% voting block and all that 25% voted their beliefs, they would carry every election and put Christians in office.

Thom Rainer, a leader in church health studies has remarked, "When the preferences of the church members are greater than their passion for the Gospel, the church is dying."

Not only are individual churches dying or seriously in trouble, most don't even realize the problem. There have been many church splits personally seen, but only one on account of false doctrine. One split was over the type of pulpit. Another was over the nursery drapes. Still another was over service times. Most were all about personal power, someone who didn't have power, wanted power.

So, what's gone wrong and how do we become THE CHURCH again? The Bible says believers will be refined as gold by fire, does that fire have to be persecution?

Many in the Church want revival, but few want to be the change. Most church members want to see folks brought into the church, but few want to say a word to their neighbor about Jesus. Most sit on their padded pew and wonder why there are so few people coming anymore, but mighty few look for a reason.

The needed change starts with the Gospel of Jesus Christ for it is the Power of God unto Salvation . . .

Salvation 101

First of all, let's clear up the basics. Salvation is the root and tree of the fruit of Christ. It is the beginning and the end, in Christ. There is no easy believeism, no custom built pathways, no commercially enhanced baptism in the Church. It is not a weak, one moment, feel good, mamby pamby, human endeavor. It's not a process. It is not a simple walk the aisle and get dunked. It is not a prayer. It is as follows.

ALL are sinners. Romans 3:23

What is sin?

1 John 3:4 says sin is the transgression of the Law.

Proverbs 14:34 says sin is a disgrace to any People.

Proverbs 21:4 says that haughty eyes and a proud heart is sin.

Proverbs 24:9 says the thought of foolishness is sin.

Romans 14:23 says whatever is not of faith is sin.

James 4:17 says knowing to do good and not doing it is sin.

1 John 5:17 hits the final nail on the head with "all unrighteousness is sin:..."

Sin is doing it your way (unrighteous) instead of God's (righteous) way. Only those deeds done God's way are righteous. The church at Ephesus in Revelation 2:1-7 was doing all the right things, but for the wrong reasons. They had forgotten their first love, Jesus, and His will.

The price (sentence in the just court of God) for our sins (failure to live up to God's standards, all unrighteousness) is DEATH – Romans 6:23

As the cons say, "Do the crime, do the time." Only this time, we are looking at multiple crimes (sin) and the time is eternity.

We cannot meet God's standards (His Glory) on our own. – Romans 3:23

We cannot be what He had planned for us on our own. – Romans 3:10-20

He has won, claimed, taken the VICTORY over sin and death. – Romans 3:24, I Corinthians 15:54-57

SALVATION (being saved from the penalty [Hell – eternal suffering] we have earned as sinners, the consequences of our sins) is by God's GRACE through faith/believe/trust in the Lord Jesus Christ, and Him alone, + or – nothing. – Ephesians 2:8-9, Romans 10:9

To add or subtract anything from that formula would ruin it. How can it be a free gift if you have to work for it, jump through hoops for it, or if God forced it on you. The first way would make Salvation a pay check and the second would make it a burden.

We cannot earn favor with God. – Romans 8:8

Once again, earning it would make it a paycheck, something we did by work. See Page XXX – Christianity is a Works Religion for more on this subject.

There are no preparatory works or prerequisite self-improvements. Come as you are and He will make the changes. – Romans 10:13, I Timothy 1:12-16

Eternal Life is the gift of God to all those who have faith/belief/trust in Christ (Salvation). – Romans 6:23

That eternal life begins the moment of belief. You are Christ's from day one and into eternity future. The challenge is to realize that and live your life in Christ.

Those who are saved, are saved and fully justified before their faith/belief/trust produces a single righteous work. – Romans 3:10-12, Ephesians 2:10

Faith/belief/trust brings about a necessary – Luke 13:3 – and true REPENTANCE– Romans 12:1-2 – (literally – a change of direction, mind, or action). This is an unconditional surrender to the Lordship of Jesus. – John 14:15, 23

When like the little child we say "Sorry" and mean it, our life in Christ begins. To be truly sorry for our sins makes us want to not do them again, ever. We turn away from our sinful lifestyle and go in His direction, living as He lived. Our thinking even becomes like He would think. – Philippians 2:5-8, Romans 12:1-2

He has made us sinless (JUSTIFIED). – Romans 3:26

Justified can be said, "Just as if I'd" never sinned. Christ took the sins of the world with Him on that cross. Your sins have been paid for and erased on the Cross of Calvary. That is God's Grace. An interesting part of this is that God forgives, forgets, and forges ahead using every one of your sins to your benefit for Him in your life from that moment on. Romans 8:28.

This brings about a serious change in behavior. The believer becomes a new person (BORN AGAIN) in Christ. – John 3:1-20, Acts 26:18-20, 2 Corinthians 5:17, Galatians 2:20-21, Ephesians 4:24

This change in behavior may not be seen by others, but it will be known in the heart of the believer. For the first time in their lives they will want to do things God's way and they will feel deep remorse and sorrow when they slip into old patterns of sin. Living like Christ becomes the guideline and the old person is soon left behind. This is sometimes called 'Newness of life."

We need the newness of life because in Salvation we have become dead to ourselves, our desires, our wants, and are living for Christ, His wants and desires. We are imitators of Christ.

Newness of life is soon seen by others and if truly lived for Christ those others will want what the new believer has, this newness of life.

Salvation brings about COMMITMENT which lasts. – 2 Corinthians 5:15, Philippians 1:6, Hebrews 11, Ephesians 4:30.

Real faith endures forever. – Philippians 1:6, Hebrews 11

BELIEVERS/CHRISTIANS (those saved by Grace) can and do sin – 1 John 1:8-10 – and wage a constant and intense war against sin in the flesh – Romans 7:13-24.

Genuine believers sometimes commit the worst of sins. – David in 2 Samuel 13

Those who turn away from the faith were never truly saved. – 1 John 2:19

There are many arguments on this topic. Many discussions have been held concerning the possibility of losing your salvation. 1 John 2:19 discusses this and when every argument is taken to the end in calm discussion, this passage stands as the proof of the idea of eternal life from the moment of first belief. If one truly believes, he or she repents, commits, and lives accordingly. If one is just trying it out to see what happens and there is no real repentance, serious commitment, or signs of a deeply changed life, they were never saved.

You can see that Salvation is easy. But, easy believeism (having a mental knowledge and understanding only) will get you in trouble. Again, it is not a walk down an aisle and getting dunked, it is not the saying of a simple prayer, it is not work hard and maybe God will like you, it is not a get rich quick scheme, it is a lifetime commitment to the Lordship of Jesus Christ with all you are, all you have, all you ever will be.

You will receive the Holy Spirit at that moment. The Holy Spirit of God was promised by Jesus as He left earth to return to the Father (Acts 1:1-9 and John 15:26-16:15).The Holy Spirit is the seal of God on/in our lives (Ephesians 4:30). The Spirit is to guide our lives (Ephesians 5:18) by testifying of Truth (Jesus) (John 15:26). The Holy Spirit will, thru you, convince (convict) the world of sin, and righteousness, and judgement. He will guide you to all Truth and Understanding (discernment). He will glorify Jesus in you. (John 16:1-16).

The Holy Spirit will give you the power to overcome sin in your life and be a witness in the lost world.

But, once you have Salvation, then what?

CHRISTIANITY

IS

A WORKS

RELIGION!

There has been much discussion lately about WORKS RELIGIONS. It generally refers to how this group and that group rely on works to achieve their highest goal. With Eastern religions a person is required to empty themselves and join the greatness of nonexistence or some such thing. With most new religions it is a matter of how much good you do, what a good person you are.

For years the Christian has been told that Christianity is not a works religion.

That is a lie. Christianity is a works religion.

Bear with me to the end, please. The difference is where we put the works in the time line and the idea of works to achieve a goal.

We must root every idea on the Bible. Every idea must hold up under the severe and loving ideals of the God as expressed by His Word, so let's go to the Word.

Isaiah 58:1-5 (ESV)

> *1 Cry aloud; do not hold back; lift up your voice like a trumpet; declare to my people their transgression, to the house of Jacob their sins.*
>
> *2 Yet they seek me daily and delight to know my ways, as if they were a nation that did righteousness and did not forsake the judgment of their God; they ask of me righteous judgments; they delight to draw near to God.*
>
> *3 Why have we fasted, and you see it not? Why have we humbled ourselves, and you take no knowledge of it?' Behold, in the day of your fast you seek your own pleasure, and oppress all your workers.*
>
> *4 Behold, you fast only to quarrel and to fight and to hit with a wicked fist. Fasting like yours this day will not make your voice to be heard on high.*
>
> *5 Is such the fast that I choose, a day for a person to humble himself? Is it to bow down his head like a reed, and to spread sackcloth and ashes under him? Will you call this a fast, and a day acceptable to the LORD?*

God literally screams at Israel for their actions, works if you will. He tells Isaiah to let his voice be heard as if it were a trumpet. Tell them that all their acts of worship (works) are wasted and empty. All they are doing is fighting amongst themselves and committing acts of false humility. Even the fasts of Israel were designed to oppress the poor and downtrodden who were already hungry. All the acts of worship, the sackcloth, the ashes, the bowing of the head, the prayer, all of it was false and worthless. Why would God say that about his people? If they are putting forth the effort to go to the Temple and worship Him, what's the problem?

Have you ever felt like that was happening in your life, your congregation's life, your denomination's life? Have you ever felt like talking to God was like talking to a blank wall or a dead phone? What's the problem?

Israel had their sins thrown in their faces by this prophet. That had to leave a spiritual bruise on the hearts of the people. What was the problem there?

Revelation 2:1-7 (ESV)

1 To the angel of the church in Ephesus write: 'The words of him who holds the seven stars in his right hand, who walks among the seven golden lampstands.

2 'I know your works, your toil and your patient endurance, and how you cannot bear with those who are evil, but have tested those who call themselves apostles and are not, and found them to be false.

3 I know you are enduring patiently and bearing up for my name's sake, and you have not grown weary.

4 But I have this against you, that you have abandoned the love you had at first.

5 Remember therefore from where you have fallen; repent, and do the works you did at first. If not, I will come to you

and remove your lampstand from its place, unless you repent.
6 Yet this you have: you hate the works of the Nicolaitans,
which I also hate.
7 He who has an ear, let him hear what the Spirit says to the
churches. To the one who
conquers I will grant to eat of the tree of life, which is in the
paradise of God.'

This is a more modern group that Christ is addressing here. The first mega-church in the world was at Ephesus. Notice that Christ praises them for their works. They are doing everything right. They are carefully watching for false teachers, false doctrine, and they hate the things that God hates. This sounds a lot like Israel in the passage from Isaiah we just looked at. God's yelling at them in the same manner. They are doing all things right, but it is all wrong. What's the problem here?

In this passage God gives us a rock solid explanation for His hard words. They are doing all the right things for all the wrong reasons. They have forgotten their first love, their love of Christ. In other words, they were doing it all for their own glory, to get their pictures on the front page of the newspaper, headlines, to chalk up points against the church across the street, to make themselves look and feel good, and not for the Glory of God.

For both of these passages of Scripture, it looks like works get you in trouble with God rather than pleasing Him. What's the problem?

I'll give you a hint, the problem is not in the doing.

Proverbs 1:20-33 (ESV)

20 Wisdom cries aloud in the street, in the markets she raises her voice;

21 at the head of the noisy streets she cries out; at the entrance of the city gates she speaks:

22 "How long, O simple ones, will you love being simple? How long will scoffers delight in their scoffing and fools hate knowledge?

23 If you turn at my reproof, behold, I will pour out my spirit to you; I will make my words known to you.

24 Because I have called and you refused to listen, have stretched out my hand and no one has heeded,

25 because you have ignored all my counsel and would have none of my reproof,

26 I also will laugh at your calamity; I will mock when terror strikes you,

27 when terror strikes you like a storm and your calamity comes like a whirlwind, when distress and anguish come upon you.

28 Then they will call upon me, but I will not answer; they will seek me diligently but will not find me.

29 Because they hated knowledge and did not choose the fear of the LORD,

30 would have none of my counsel and despised all my reproof,

31 Therefore they shall eat the fruit of their way, and have their fill of their own devices.

32 For the simple are killed by their turning away, and the complacency of fools destroys them;
33 but whoever listens to me will dwell secure and will be at ease, without dread of disaster."

This is the scariest passage in all of Scripture. It scares me more than the fires of Hell.

God calls out to man and man refuses to answer, comply, or do. What does God do after making all these various efforts? He doesn't listen to them. He won't hear them when they call. We complain when God appears to not answer our prayers and then begin to question His purpose. The purpose is never in God's response or lack of response. Even when he answers with "no" or "wait," He is answering. If there is total silence, there just might be a problem on your end.

There is a story of an old rancher in Wyoming that makes a point here. The old rancher is out checking on his cows, miles away from anything. A snow storm is moving in on him and he decides he better get to home before the snow gets too deep. He walks to his truck and it won't start. Everything looks good under the hood. There is gas in the tank. He tries again. Still nothing. The rancher huddles in the cab with his blanket up around his ears as the snow piles up around his truck and he prays. He prayed until he died from the cold. Next thing he knows, he's at the Golden Gates talking with God. He asks, "How come you didn't start my truck like I asked?" God answered, "I hadn't heard your voice or seen you in my house for so long I didn't recognize who was calling. I started the truck for a long haul driver in East Texas."

Dumb joke, but would God recognize your voice if you called? Do you recognize His voice when he calls?

My book THE FISHY PROPHET is a good study in calls.

1 Corinthians 11:17-22 (ESV)

17 But in the following instructions I do not commend you, because when you come together it is not for the better but for the worse.

18 For, in the first place, when you come together as a church, I hear that there are divisions among you. And I believe it in part,

19 for there must be factions among you in order that those who are genuine among you may be recognized.

20 When you come together, it is not the Lord's supper that you eat.

21 For in eating, each one goes ahead with his own meal. One goes hungry, another gets drunk.

22 What! Do you not have houses to eat and drink in? Or do you despise the church of God and humiliate those who have nothing? What shall I say to you? Shall I commend you in this? No, I will not.

Once again we see the church doing right things and yet are condemned because they do them for the wrong reasons. They are celebrating the Lord's Supper, In Remembrance Of Me, and yet Paul is led to write, "Shall I commend you in this? No, I will not."

All this we have covered so far is about works, tasks God has commanded we do, but in the doing the individuals are in the wrong. Where's the problem?

The first thing that a person, congregation, denomination must do is truly get right with God.

Ephesians 2:8-10 (ESV)

> *8 For by grace you have been saved through faith. And this is not your own doing; it is the gift of God,*
> *9 not a result of works, so that no one may boast.*
> *10 For we are his workmanship, created in Christ Jesus for good works, which God prepared beforehand, that we should walk in them.*

You have probably heard this group of verses many times. Although, most folks leave off verse 10, 8 and 9 provide the basis for our salvation and rightness with God. There is no other way to become righteous in God's eyes except by the tenets of these three verses.

See SALVATION 101 – page XXXX

Works will not save you from the just punishment of a Holy God. The statement is that only God's Grace + your faith + or – nothing else = Rightness with God, Salvation (being saved from the just punishment of a Holy God). Grace was taken care of at the Cross of Calvary, bought and paid for by the blood of the Lamb, Jesus, Messiah. Salvation is by faith and faith alone.

Let me say that again. Salvation is by faith and faith alone.

With that said, look at verse 10. We are HIS workmanship, masterpiece, work of art, created in Christ Jesus, the image of God, for the purpose of GOOD WORKS which God has prepared for us to do. Salvation is by faith and faith alone, and out of Salvation come works.

Let's take a look at what those works might be. We'll start with an oft quoted verse or two, and look at God's response if possible.

2 Chronicles 7:12-16 (ESV)

> *12 Then the LORD appeared to Solomon in the night and said to him: "I have heard your prayer and have chosen this place for myself as a house of sacrifice.*
>
> *13 When I shut up the heavens so that there is no rain, or command the locust to devour the land, or send pestilence among my people,*
>
> *14 if my people who are called by my name humble themselves, and pray and seek my face and turn from their wicked ways, then I will hear from heaven and will forgive their sin and heal their land.*
>
> *15 Now my eyes will be open and my ears attentive to the prayer that is made in this place.*
>
> *16 For now I have chosen and consecrated this house that my name may be there forever. My eyes and my heart will be there for all time.*

Solomon built a beautiful Temple as a home to the God of Israel. He worries that God may not find it adequate because of the sins of

Israel. In Solomon's troubled sleep God comes to him and gives him this message. God tells Solomon that when trouble comes to Israel, they have to do, TO DO, a couple of works.

The first is get humble. The second and third and fourth go together, pray and seek HIS face and turn from their wicked ways. When trouble comes works are required. The works probably don't seem like much, but look again. The nation must get humble (Israel is unable to fix the problem – a terribly humbling realization). They must pray (asking God for forgiveness and help). They must seek (pursue, go after, beg for) the presence of God. Then comes the hard part, they must repent (turn away from sin, unrighteousness) from their wicked ways. The entire nation must be involved.

No easy works there. Each of the works required brings them closer to Almighty God. We are not talking about some rote prayer said over and over. Nor are we talking of asking for forgiveness without a willingness to feel the humiliation due their error in judgment. It isn't a gimme prayer; it is a heartfelt, body wrenching, heartbroken cry prayer. It is the sincere sorrow and anguish prayer that causes one to vow from the depths of their being to change and go in a different direction, repentance. Paul calls it Godly Sorrow in 2 Corinthians 9:10.

God says to them that when all this happens He will hear, forgive, and heal the land.

Isaiah 58:6-14 (ESV)

> 6 *"Is not this the fast that I choose: to loose the bonds of wickedness, to undo the straps of the yoke, to let the oppressed go free, and to break every yoke?*

7 Is it not to share your bread with the hungry and bring the homeless poor into your house; when you see the naked, to cover him, and not to hide yourself from your own flesh?

8 Then shall your light break forth like the dawn, and your healing shall spring up speedily; your righteousness shall go before you; the glory of the LORD shall be your rear guard.

9 Then you shall call, and the LORD will answer; you shall cry, and he will say, 'Here I am.' If you take away the yoke from your midst, the pointing of the finger, and speaking wickedness,

10 if you pour yourself out for the hungry and satisfy the desire of the afflicted, then shall your light rise in the darkness and your gloom be as the noonday.

11 And the LORD will guide you continually and satisfy your desire in scorched places and make your bones strong; and you shall be like a watered garden, like a spring of water, whose waters do not fail.

12 And your ancient ruins shall be rebuilt; you shall raise up the foundations of many generations; you shall be called the repairer of the breach, the restorer of streets to dwell in.

13 "If you turn back your foot from the Sabbath, from doing your pleasure on my holy day, and call the Sabbath a delight and the holy day of the LORD honorable; if you honor it, not going your own ways, or seeking your own pleasure, or talking idly;

14 then you shall take delight in the LORD, and I will make you ride on the heights of the earth; I will feed you with the heritage of Jacob your father, for the mouth of the LORD has spoken."

This passage is the continuation of the first passage we discussed in this topic.

God said that Israel was pleasing herself and not Him. Now he says to them that this is what he wants. He wants works of righteousness from His people because they are His people, called according to His purposes. (Romans 8:28) Let's list HIS works that HE wants done from this passage:

❖ Loose the bonds of wickedness

❖ Undo the straps of the yoke

❖ Let the oppressed go free

❖ Break every yoke

❖ Share your bread

❖ Bring the homeless poor to your house

❖ Cloth the naked

❖ Take care of your family (flesh)

❖ He wants these done freely, with joy, and in His name.

This is the Old Testament and maybe you think this doesn't apply today. Read on.

Matthew 25:31-46 (ESV)

31 "When the Son of Man comes in his glory, and all the angels with him, then he will sit on his glorious throne.

32 Before him will be gathered all the nations, and he will separate people one from another as a shepherd separates the sheep from the goats.

33 And he will place the sheep on his right, but the goats on the left.

34 Then the King will say to those on his right, 'Come, you who are blessed by my Father, inherit the kingdom prepared for you from the foundation of the world.

35 For I was hungry and you gave me food, I was thirsty and you gave me drink, I was a stranger and you welcomed me,

36 I was naked and you clothed me, I was sick and you visited me, I was in prison and you came to me.'

37 Then the righteous will answer him, saying, 'Lord, when did we see you hungry and feed you, or thirsty and give you drink?

38 And when did we see you a stranger and welcome you, or naked and clothe you?

39 And when did we see you sick or in prison and visit you?'

40 And the King will answer them, 'Truly, I say to you, as you did it to one of the least of these my brothers, you did it to me.'

41 "Then he will say to those on his left, 'Depart from me, you cursed, into the eternal fire prepared for the devil and his angels.

42 For I was hungry and you gave me no food, I was thirsty and you gave me no drink,

43 I was a stranger and you did not welcome me, naked and you did not clothe me, sick and in prison and you did not visit me.'

44 Then they also will answer, saying, 'Lord, when did we see you hungry or thirsty or a stranger or naked or sick or in prison, and did not minister to you?'

45 Then he will answer them, saying, 'Truly, I say to you, as you did not do it to one of the least of these, you did not do it to me.'

46 And these will go away into eternal punishment, but the righteous into eternal life."

What do we see here?

- ❖ Feed the hungry

- ❖ Water to the thirsty

- ❖ Hospitality

- ❖ Covering the naked

- ❖ Visiting the sick, compassion

- ❖ Visiting the prisoner, comfort

Jesus is saying, "You did this to the least significant of people willingly, generously, and freely. You brought me Glory. I give you eternal life with me."

Don't jump on me here. Ephesians 2:8-10 applies first. ALL OF OUR WORKS MUST BE OUT OF FAITH.

Romans 14:23

"What is not of faith is sin."

A man or woman can do many wild and wonderful things and still go to Hell. Our works must come out of faith in Christ, not into or to earn salvation (I did all this, so now I am a good person and going to Heaven with God).

So, thus far we have seen some blunt statements concerning salvation and works, and the relationship between them. Let's look at some other works that God wants out of us because we are saved.

James 1:19-27 (ESV)

19 Know this, my beloved brothers: let every person be quick to hear, slow to speak, slow to anger;

20 for the anger of man does not produce the righteousness of God.

21 Therefore put away all filthiness and rampant wickedness and receive with meekness the implanted word, which is able to save your souls.

22 But be doers of the word, and not hearers only, deceiving yourselves.

23 For if anyone is a hearer of the word and not a doer, he is like a man who looks intently at his natural face in a mirror.

24 For he looks at himself and goes away and at once forgets what he was like.

25 But the one who looks into the perfect law, the law of liberty, and perseveres, being no hearer who forgets but a doer who acts, he will be blessed in his doing.

26 If anyone thinks he is religious and does not bridle his tongue but deceives his heart, this person's religion is worthless.

27 Religion that is pure and undefiled before God, the Father, is this: to visit orphans and widows in their affliction, and to keep oneself unstained from the world.

A new list of works to look at:

- ❖ Quick to hear, slow to speak, and slow to anger

- ❖ Eliminate all evil and wrong actions

- ❖ Take the Word to heart

- ❖ Be doers of the Word (Keep Jesus' commandments)

- ❖ Keep control of your words

- ❖ Visit the orphans and widows relieving their trials

- ❖ Don't be influenced by the world's ideas

Look at verse 22. Be doers of the Word and not one who only hears. One who hears only and does not do (work) is deceiving themself. The Doer will be blessed in his doing (vs. 25). The one who is not a doer of the Word forgets who he is in Christ.

All these works boil down to two rules:

1. Love God

2. Love everybody else   (Mark 12:29-31)

Notice that "ME" is out of the picture here. Yes, you are to love others as you love yourself, but the emphasis is on the others, not yourself.

How does that settle with you?

James 2:18-23 (ESV)

18 But someone will say, "You have faith and I have works." Show me your faith apart from your works, and I will show you my faith by my works.

19 You believe that God is one; you do well. Even the demons believe—and shudder!

20 Do you want to be shown, you foolish person, that faith apart from works is useless?

21 Was not Abraham our father justified by works when he offered up his son Isaac on the altar?

22 You see that faith was active along with his works, and faith was completed by his works;

23 and the Scripture was fulfilled that says, "Abraham believed God, and it was counted to him as righteousness"— and he was called a friend of God.

You can say you have faith all you want and do nothing. If you are that kind of person it will be impossible to tell what you believe and why or for whom. If you have faith and do the works the Lord has commanded, some of which we have seen above, then folks will know you truly believe in Christ by those works. There are no secret service agents in the Body of Christ.

Let me say something cautiously and praying that you will hear and know the love and concern I have for all people as I say it. If your faith is not seen in your day to day actions, I have some serious doubts about your salvation. What we believe we live and advertise. What we believe we will try to sell to others. What we believe will be seen in every aspect of our lives. What we believe will never be hidden from those around us. What do your observers see?

I pray that if you were accused of being a Christian, you would be proclaimed guilty by everyone you come in contact with. You can carry a Bible with you every day and never be seen to be a Christian. You have to live the Bible every day to be convicted, and that my brothers and sisters, is work.

In verses19-22 James leads us through this idea by showing that Abraham did all he did because he believed in God. In so doing (works) he proved his faith and was counted, labeled, called righteous by God.

John 14:12-14 (ESV)

12 "Truly, truly, I say to you, whoever believes in me will also do the works that I do; and greater works than these will he do, because I am going to the Father.

13 Whatever you ask in my name, this I will do, that the Father may be glorified in the Son.

14 If you ask me anything in my name, I will do it.

What conditions do you see here?

How can you get what you ask for?

From the lips of Jesus we are told that we, you and me, because of faith, will do greater works than He did, because we can call on the same power He did. If you ask for that power in Jesus' name (for His glory and reputation) it will be done (work). This passage has been tossed around for countless years and we forget it because it sounds like way too much to expect. We are so sophisticated and scientific we don't believe in miracles anymore. Let me tell you one thing here and now, "That is not so. Miracles are a daily thing, we just don't see them. We write them off to all our modern wisdom. The Bible says that man, professing himself to be wise, is a fool."

I have a quote I wrote down not too long ago. I do not remember who said it or where I heard it. It goes, "We have small influence because we live a small life believing in a small God."

Do you agree or disagree with that? Explain.

Take a look at Isaiah 43 to get a picture of how big God is.
John 14:15-24 (ESV)

> 15 "If you love me, you will keep my commandments.
> 16 And I will ask the Father, and he will give you another Helper, to be with you forever,

17 even the Spirit of truth, whom the world cannot receive, because it neither sees him nor knows him. You know him, for he dwells with you and will be in you.

18 "I will not leave you as orphans; I will come to you.

19 Yet a little while and the world will see me no more, but you will see me. Because I live, you also will live.

20 In that day you will know that I am in my Father, and you in me, and I in you.

21 Whoever has my commandments and keeps them, he it is who loves me. And he who loves me will be loved by my Father, and I will love him and manifest myself to him."

22 Judas (not Iscariot) said to him, "Lord, how is it that you will manifest yourself to us, and not to the world?"

23 Jesus answered him, "If anyone loves me, he will keep my word, and my Father will love him, and we will come to him and make our home with him.

24 Whoever does not love me does not keep my words. And the word that you hear is not mine but the Father's who sent me.

Jesus' words again. He says the same thing James said. Only he says it, "If you love Me, do what I say." The key words here are if and do. The doing shows the focus of our love. Does your life show a focus of a love for Christ? This same condition applies to the indwelling of the Holy Spirit. Verse 16 adds that because of our obedience out of love we will get the Holy Spirit as a gift from the

Father. Do this to get that, condition and promise, the pattern of God's law in the Bible.

Notice in verse 21 that there is a difference between knowing, having, learning the commandments, and keeping them. The one that keeps the commandments is the one that loves Christ, and will be loved by Him and made known to Him.

Then in verse 23 Jesus says the one that loves Him will be obedient and because of that will be loved by the Father and the Godhead will make their home with the obedient one. Could it be that we live a small life in the church because we have no one home with us? If that is true we do not have salvation and we can't do anything to God's Glory because we don't have Him. To steal a phase we use for some people, "the lights are on, but no one is home." Only in this case there is no light inside so there can be no illumination of the world around us.

Matthew 5:14-16 (ESV)

14 "You are the light of the world. A city set on a hill cannot be hidden.

15 Nor do people light a lamp and put it under a basket, but on a stand, and it gives light to all in the house.

16 In the same way, let your light shine before others, so that they may see your good works and give glory to your Father who is in heaven.

Verse 16 is my life verse. I paraphrase and personalize it in the front of all my journals. It goes "Let my life so shine before those

WHAT OUGHT TO BE

around me so they may see the good works that I do and give all Glory to God and, hopefully, come to Christ."

We are supposed to do good works. We are commanded to do good works. Jesus said in John 10:25 that his works were his credentials as the Messiah. Our good works are our credentials as the sons and daughters of the one true God.

James 4:17 (ESV)

17 So whoever knows the right thing to do and fails to do it, for him it is sin.

This is a loaded statement. How do you see yourself with this verse?

When we know the good work that is needed and don't perform it, we sin.

Ephesians 4:7-16 (ESV)

7 But grace was given to each one of us according to the measure of Christ's gift.

8 Therefore it says, "When he ascended on high he led a host of captives, and he gave gifts to men."

9 (In saying, "He ascended," what does it mean but that he had also descended into the lower regions, the earth?

10 He who descended is the one who also ascended far above all the heavens, that he might fill all things.)

11 And he gave the apostles, the prophets, the evangelists, the shepherds and teachers,

12 to equip the saints for the work of ministry, for building up the body of Christ,

13 until we all attain to the unity of the faith and of the knowledge of the Son of God, to mature manhood, to the measure of the stature of the fullness of Christ,

14 so that we may no longer be children, tossed to and fro by the waves and carried about by every wind of doctrine, by human cunning, by craftiness in deceitful schemes.

15 Rather, speaking the truth in love, we are to grow up in every way into him who is the head, into Christ,

16 from whom the whole body, joined and held together by every joint with which it is equipped, when each part is working properly, makes the body grow so that it builds itself up in love.

What is the measure of Christ's gift? He gave up His life. He gave up all for us. He asks no more and no less of us.

We all have gifts. We all have good works to do with them. All the gifts and the works are to build up the Body of Christ.

Let me end this with one more statement I heard and cannot remember the reference. It goes, "What would my church be like if all the members were just like me?"

What would your church be like if all the members were just like YOU?

Good Works
Part 2

Matthew 28:18-20 (ESV)

18 And Jesus came and said to them, "All authority in heaven and on earth has been given to me.

19 Go therefore and make disciples of all nations, baptizing them in the name of the Father and of the Son and of the Holy Spirit,

20 teaching them to observe all that I have commanded you. And behold, I am with you always, to the end of the age."

Most of the folks that go to church have heard this passage more than twice. It is called "The Great Commission." It calls for a lot of work, hard work, tough work, and in some cases deadly work.

What's your piece of this work?

This is the controlling purpose, command to, the Church, The Body of Christ, you, and me. We cannot choose just one factor in the Commission and reject the rest, but must work faithfully focused on the entire command. This is a Commission: Co – together, and mission – focused task. We are to be on a mission, a focused task, together with Christ.

We are commanded to GO. It's a command. An imperative statement. Some even interpret it as 'AS YOU GO' to include all moments in our lives and I can agree with that.

But, notice, before He commands us to GO, he states, *"All power has been given to me on earth and in heaven."* That leaves nowhere out. Jesus has ALL power and is giving it to us to do the mission at hand, the focused task for us to do together with Him.

Then you'll notice that this commission covers the entire earth. It's not just your house, or your church, or your neighborhood, it's the whole world. We are told to focus first on the home and then further and further away until all the world is affected by His power. We are never told to be missions minded, that is sitting in the pew and thinking about missions. We are told to be missional, which is to be always on the task of making disciples and baptizing new members into the Kingdom of God. Missional is a total focus on the mission at all times.

Then we are to teach. Teach what? Teach them everything you know. If you only know John 3:16, teach them that. If you know the etymology of the entire Bible, teach that. Teaching means to bring to understanding, in this case to bring the whole world to an understanding of all God is about and who Christ is.

What do you know that you should be teaching?

Much of our teaching is by example and not by words of our mouth. I remember reading a book *RIGHT FROM WRONG* by Josh McDowell where he tells the story of a father who comes home to find out his son has been caught lying in school and was sent home.

The mother is all teary as the dad takes the son to the dining room table for one of those chats. At the end, after two hours, the father says to the son, "Do you understand how important it is to never tell a lie and to always be truthful even if it hurts?" The son agrees. They stand and head for the den with the phone rings. The son is closest to it. He reaches for the phone. The father says, "If it's for me, tell them I'm not here."

Which part of that evening's discussion will be remembered?

We teach and learn by the examples around us.

Our command in the Word (Eph 5:1) is to be imitators of God. As an imitator our lives will show the love of God and all the other attributes that drew us to Him.

Baptizing is to immerse, to immerse folks in the entirety of Christ.

Romans 6:1-14 (ESV)

> *1 What shall we say then? Are we to continue in sin that grace may abound?*
>
> *2 By no means! How can we who died to sin still live in it?*
>
> *3 Do you not know that all of us who have been baptized into Christ Jesus were baptized into his death?*
>
> *4 We were buried therefore with him by baptism into death, in order that, just as Christ was raised from the dead by the glory of the Father, we too might walk in newness of life.*
>
> *5 For if we have been united with him in a death like his, we shall certainly be united with him in a resurrection like his.*

6 We know that our old self was crucified with him in order that the body of sin might be brought to nothing, so that we would no longer be enslaved to sin.

7 For one who has died has been set free from sin.

8 Now if we have died with Christ, we believe that we will also live with him.

9 We know that Christ, being raised from the dead, will never die again; death no longer has dominion over him.

10 For the death he died he died to sin, once for all, but the life he lives he lives to God.

11 So you also must consider yourselves dead to sin and alive to God in Christ Jesus.

12 Let not sin therefore reign in your mortal body, to make you obey its passions.

13 Do not present your members to sin as instruments for unrighteousness, but present yourselves to God as those who have been brought from death to life, and your members to God as instruments for righteousness.

14 For sin will have no dominion over you, since you are not under law but under grace.

We see from this passage that baptism is representative of Christ's death, burial, and resurrection. We are immersed as into the grave. We rise up from the grave a new person in Christ. Our death is a death to self (Luke 9:23, Romans 12:1-2) and our resurrection is to a new life (2 Cor 5:17, Gal 6:15), a life lived for Christ who died for us. (Galatians 2:20-21)

Jesus says that they have all His power and then says, "I am with you always." So, not only is the power a part of us, but He is also with us in the mission at all moments, in all situations, and for all power. He is our authority, our power, our example. So we evangelize, baptize, and disciplize. Many believers and churches forget that last one.

Even to the end of the age is the limit of this command. The end of the age will see the end of our works.

If we carried out this religiously, with the assumption there are 1.5 billion Christians on the face of the earth, and each of us led one person a year to Christ, in one year we would have 3 billion believers and after 2 there would be 6. After the middle of February of the third year there would be no one to lead to Christ. If we start with only 94 million, it would still only take 6 years.

Ezekiel 3:16-21 (ESV)

16 And at the end of seven days, the word of the LORD came to me:

17 "Son of man, I have made you a watchman for the house of Israel. Whenever you hear a word from my mouth, you shall give them warning from me.

18 If I say to the wicked, 'You shall surely die,' and you give him no warning, nor speak to warn the wicked from his wicked way, in order to save his life, that wicked person shall die for his iniquity, but his blood I will require at your hand.

19 But if you warn the wicked, and he does not turn from his wickedness, or from his wicked way, he shall die for his iniquity, but you will have delivered your soul.

20 Again, if a righteous person turns from his righteousness and commits injustice, and I lay a stumbling block before him, he shall die. Because you have not warned him, he shall die for his sin, and his righteous deeds that he has done shall not be remembered, but his blood I will require at your hand. 21 But if you warn the righteous person not to sin, and he does not sin, he shall surely live, because he took warning, and you will have delivered your soul."

Does this apply to us? If someone goes to hell are we held accountable? Just a thought. It is what we are commanded to do, is it not?

WHOSE BLOOD IS ON YOUR HANDS?

We all know, or should know, that it is the blood, the sacrifice, of Christ that offers us this great opportunity of being right with God, being saved from the consequences of our sins, being able to belong to the family of God. But, what about your blood?

Ezekiel 3:16-21 (KJV)

16 And it came to pass at the end of seven days, that the word of the LORD came unto me, saying,

17 Son of man, I have made thee a watchman unto the house of Israel: therefore hear the word at my mouth, and give them warning from me.

18 When I say unto the wicked, Thou shalt surely die; and thou givest him not warning, nor speakest to warn the wicked from his wicked way, to save his life; the same wicked man shall die in his iniquity; but his blood will I require at thine hand.

19 Yet if thou warn the wicked, and he turn not from his wickedness, nor from his wicked way, he shall die in his iniquity; but thou hast delivered thy soul.

20 Again, when a righteous man doth turn from his righteousness, and commit iniquity, and I lay a stumblingblock before him, he shall die: because thou hast not given him warning, he shall die in his sin, and his righteousness which he hath done shall not be remembered; but his blood will I require at thine hand.

21 Nevertheless if thou warn the righteous man, that the righteous sin not, and he doth not sin, he shall surely live, because he is warned; also thou hast delivered thy soul.

This is the passage we left off with as we talked of WORKS. Have you thought on it any at all? Or, did you brush it off and as not applicable to your situation?

Old Zeke is in a fix. God called him to do a job. God laid on him a burden. He has been locked up, told to lie down on one side, cook his food over a dung fire, and now He says to Zeke that if he doesn't do his works that God has laid down for him, he will have blood on his hands. He will be the cause of folks going to Hell. Their blood will be required of Ezekiel.

Does that apply to us? Is this part of the Great Commission? If we don't witness, make disciples, teach, and baptize will the blood of men be on our hands?

I read this in my devotions and wondered about it. Does this apply today? I searched the Word.

Let's read on.

You decide.

Acts 18:6 (KJV)

6 And when they opposed themselves, and blasphemed, he shook his raiment, and said unto them, Your blood be upon your own heads; I am clean: from henceforth I will go unto the Gentiles.

Paul tries to teach and disciple, but the people do not listen. They worked against their own salvation. They blasphemed (Did they blaspheme the Holy Spirit?). Paul says he is clean, their blood is not his responsibility. He would go to others who will listen.

Acts 20:26-28 (KJV)

26 Wherefore I take you to record this day, that I am pure from the blood of all men.

27 For I have not shunned to declare unto you all the counsel of God.

28 Take heed therefore unto yourselves, and to all the flock, over the which the Holy Ghost hath made you overseers, to feed the church of God, which he hath purchased with his own blood.

Paul says here that he is pure, clean of the blood of all men because he has witnessed, declared the Word to them. Then he warns all the listeners to take heed, pay attention to the feeding of the Church, all the Church. The feeding is the declaration of all the counsel of God. Tell folks the whole story, all of it, not just what you like.

1 Timothy 4:16 (KJV)

16 Take heed unto thyself, and unto the doctrine; continue in them: for in doing this thou shalt both save thyself, and them that hear thee.

Here Paul tells Timothy that he must continue to teach doctrine and keep teaching the whole Gospel in order to save himself and the ones who hear him. That almost sounds like if we don't teach the Word we aren't really saved ourselves doesn't it?

Ezekiel 14:14 (KJV)

14 Though these three men, Noah, Daniel, and Job, were in it, they should deliver but their own souls by their righteousness, saith the Lord GOD.

The simple statement here is that each man or woman, powerful or weak, known or obscure must decide on their own whether to follow Christ or not. Someone can teach all day, but it is the hearer's responsibility to learn and decide what they will do with the new knowledge.

Isaiah 49:3-5 (KJV)

3 And said unto me, Thou art my servant, O Israel, in whom I will be glorified.

4 Then I said, I have laboured in vain, I have spent my strength for nought, and in vain: yet surely my judgment is with the LORD, and my work with my God.

5 And now, saith the LORD that formed me from the womb to be his servant, to bring Jacob again to him, Though Israel be not gathered, yet shall I be glorious in the eyes of the LORD, and my God shall be my strength.

WHAT OUGHT TO BE

Isaiah was given the work of proclaiming repentance before a Holy God to all of Israel. He did it. Here he tells them that he did his job, work, before God and therefore he is innocent of anything that might happen to the ones who chose not to listen. He even says he is glorious in the eyes of the Lord because he did his work, job, task, assignment.

Isaiah 50:4 (KJV)

4 The Lord GOD hath given me the tongue of the learned, that I should know how to speak a word in season to him that is weary: he wakeneth morning by morning, he wakeneth mine ear to hear as the learned.

This verse intrigues me. Isaiah says that God has given him the tongue in his head to present the Word and that God wakes him up every morning to do his task. Did you wake up this morning? Are you able to speak?

Ezekiel 18:21-28 (KJV)

21 But if the wicked will turn from all his sins that he hath committed, and keep all my statutes, and do that which is lawful and right, he shall surely live, he shall not die.

22 All his transgressions that he hath committed, they shall not be mentioned unto him: in his righteousness that he hath done he shall live.

23 Have I any pleasure at all that the wicked should die? saith the Lord GOD: and not that he should return from his ways, and live?

24 But when the righteous turneth away from his righteousness, and committeth iniquity, and doeth according to all the abominations that the wicked man doeth, shall he live? All his righteousness that he hath done shall not be mentioned: in his trespass that he hath trespassed, and in his sin that he hath sinned, in them shall he die.

25 Yet ye say, The way of the Lord is not equal. Hear now, O house of Israel; Is not my way equal? are not your ways unequal?

26 When a righteous man turneth away from his righteousness, and committeth iniquity, and dieth in them; for his iniquity that he hath done shall he die.

27 Again, when the wicked man turneth away from his wickedness that he hath committed, and doeth that which is lawful and right, he shall save his soul alive.

28 Because he considereth, and turneth away from all his transgressions that he hath committed, he shall surely live, he shall not die.

Once again we see that the decision belongs to the individual hearing the Word. We also hear that some person is designated to present the Word to each and every person. The Word is to be presented by the called one, believer, and the one that hears/sees the presentation is responsible for their own reaction to the presentation.

Psalm 125:5 (KJV)

5 As for such as turn aside unto their crooked ways, the LORD shall lead them forth with the workers of iniquity: but peace shall be upon Israel.

Those who hear the presentation and then turn aside shall be treated as workers of iniquity, sinners, but the ones who follow are Israel and His people. They are doing well.

1 John 1:8-10 (KJV)

8 If we say that we have no sin, we deceive ourselves, and the truth is not in us.

9 If we confess our sins, he is faithful and just to forgive us our sins, and to cleanse us from all unrighteousness.

10 If we say that we have not sinned, we make him a liar, and his word is not in us.

John tells us that because 'all have sinned' it is up to each individual to admit to that sin and be cleansed. To not do so makes that person a liar and God's Word, the Gospel, is not in, does not apply to that person. Once we admit our sins through confession (which includes repentance and genuine sorrow) He is faithful, He will keep His promise, and forgive/cleanse us of that sin.

1 John 2:19 (KJV)

19 They went out from us, but they were not of us; for if they had been of us, they would no doubt have continued with us: but they went out, that they might be made manifest that they were not all of us.

This passage is one that answers a lot of questions. A person who has received the Word of the Gospel and appeared to respond positively (be saved) who leaves the Body of Christ to return to his old ways was never saved to begin with, was never a part of the Body of Christ. That person left to show he was not a part of the Body of Christ.

A bit of a tangent here, how often do we spend hours and days chasing people who have been in the church for years, but are now not involved and want nothing to do with it, and off we go working hard to get them to return? Many hearts have been broken by the ones that have left the fellowship and show they were never really a part of it. They know better in their heads, why are we still trying to talk them into coming back to pollute the fellowship? If they are willing to repent, great, but otherwise let God deal with them.

We are at the end of this topic. You have read the passages. You have read my comments. Is the blood of the lost people that you come in contact with on your hands if you do not present the Word to them?

I think it is.

Ezekiel, Isaiah, and Jeremiah were told none would respond.

We are told some will.

UNITY

Our monotheistic traditions reinforce the assumption that the Universe is at root a unity, that it is not governed by a different legislation in different places, neither the residue of some clash of Titans wrestling to impose their arbitrary wills upon the nature of things, nor the compromise of some cosmic committees.

John D. Barrow, New Theories of Everything, 2007, Pg 18

I believe just the opposite has happened. Our monotheistic traditions have caused us to choose up sides within the tradition and split ourselves into so many legislative groups we are worthless. Denominationalism has destroyed our oneness in Christ. We spend more time arguing with each other over the picky little details of our own personal understandings, which weak due to our human limitations, and thereby lose the power of the many. If we quit fighting amongst ourselves and turn to fight the enemy, Satan, we would have a powerful impact with the power of the Lord on our side.

Picture a football game, or any team sport, where every player has his or her own agenda playing against a modern, unified, coached team of players. On every play the non-unified team goes in 9 different directions and runs their own pattern. Each player wants to be play caller and thinks their way is the only way that's right.

A team in pieces like that wins nothing and goes nowhere.

Picture a town of 13,000 people. In that town there are 16 evangelical churches professing and proclaiming Christ. Each of them has sound doctrine as their core, but each has one picky little point of doctrine or worship that makes them different. Whether it be mode of baptism, gifts, or music, they spend their focus on trying to convince each other and the community they are the right way and the best church – COME JOIN US.

Bars, drugs, and crime run rampant in the streets. Children are coerced into drugs. Women are assaulted. It isn't safe on the streets at night. Racism runs rampant. The government is corrupt. But, no, they are too busy fighting each other to address the lost and dying, going to Hell folks that live next door.

This must stop. The Bible says so.

1 Corinthians 1:10-13 (ESV)

> *I appeal to you, brothers, by the name of our Lord Jesus Christ, that all of you agree, and that there be no divisions among you, but that you be united in the same mind and the same judgment. For it has been reported to me by Chloe's people that there is quarreling among you, my brothers. What I mean is that each one of you says, "I follow Paul," or "I follow Apollos," or "I follow Cephas," or "I follow Christ." Is Christ divided? Was Paul crucified for you? Or were you baptized in the name of Paul.*

Paul writing to the church at Corinth under the leading of the Holy Spirit appeals to all Christians in the strongest terms possible to eliminate divisions within the church body.

The first Pastor I ever sat under, that I remember listening to, said that the Epistles to the Corinthians were the best church governance guidelines ever written and applied to churches of all ages because the church at Corinth had every problem that a church could have. The people were a great cross section of the people of all ages, the warfare within the church was the warfare of the ages, and the focus of the people was the same as the focus of churches of all ages. In other words, if you've seen First Church of Corinth, you've seen them all.

Here was a church that was divided, on at least one issue, by who baptized them. Our churches today argue over what baptism is (Immersed in the Holy Spirit, Water, or Christ), who it is for (New believers, rededication, ordination), how it is done (Sprinkle, Immersion, complete/total/every spot covered, private, public), who can do it (Clergy, elders, anyone), and what it does (Public profession, joining the church, washes away original or all sin, and/or demonstrates obedience). One says the baptism is the baptism of the Holy Spirit, another says it is the sprinkling of water on infants or new members, another is dogmatic on the complete immersion of the whole body of the person at the same time.

Is it really that important?

Yes. Baptism is important. But, which Baptism?

Should that point alone divide us?

No. Baptism is important, but is it the focal point of the Church?

Some folks say that if you walk the aisle or say a little prayer and get baptized you have your place in heaven assured; while others believe you must make a serious commitment and keep that commitment for the rest of your life.

Look at the thief next to Christ. All he had was a few hours of agony, not for his stand for the Lord, but for his crimes. He professed Christ in public and Christ said that was enough. If he was baptized, it was in physical darkness, rain (?), and/or the Holy Spirit.

If we look at this scene even closer we find that he didn't need baptism. His faith was the faith of the Old Testament believers. There was no death, burial, and resurrection, Christ was still alive on the cross next to him. Romans 6 did not yet apply.

On Christ's death, burial, and resurrection there was a shift from belief in the coming Messiah to the Grace of the New Testament which in many cases has become an industrial product brightly packaged grace that never approaches the real Grace of Christ's death, burial, and resurrection into new life and a new person. God's Grace is a promise of transformation, redemption, sanctification, and reconciliation into Good Works prepared for the transformed by God from before the foundations of the earth were in place. (Ephesians 2:10)

Strong's Concordance of the Bible states Bapto-a primary verb, to whelm. Webster says: vt. 1. To submerge, cover, or engulf; 2. To overpower or crush, overwhelm.

That said, Baptism is an important part of the life of the Church. But, what is it? Romans 6 shows it as a symbol of the death, burial, and resurrection of Christ. The Word states the following.

Acts 2:37-41 (KJV)

Now when they heard this, they were pricked in their heart, and said unto Peter and to the rest of the apostles, Men and brethren, what shall we do? Then Peter said unto them, Repent, and be baptized every one of you in the name of Jesus Christ for the remission of sins, and ye shall receive the gift of the Holy Ghost. For the promise is unto you, and to your children, and to all that are afar off, even as many as the Lord our God shall call. And with many other words did he testify and exhort, saying, Save yourselves from this untoward generation. Then they that gladly received his word were baptized: and the same day there were added unto them about three thousand souls.

In Acts 1:8 the people who waited in the Upper Room were promised that they would receive power when the Holy Spirit was given to them. The results of that reception were the miracle of folks hearing in their own tongue the joy of belief and the power of the reception of the Spirit. There is no indication that those in the upper room, including Peter, were ever baptized for their belief in Christ in any way other than the reception (baptism, imersion) of the Holy Spirit at Pentecost. They could have been a part of the 3,000 new believers who saw the results of the Holy Spirit and who got baptized on Pentecost, or not.

Acts 10:46-48 (KJV)

For they heard them speak with tongues, and magnify God. Then answered Peter, Can any man forbid water, that these

*should not be baptized, which have received the Holy Ghost
as well as we? And he commanded them to be baptized in the
name of the Lord. Then prayed they him to tarry certain
days.*

Again the speaking in tongues before baptism. Peter even
commands their baptism in water for them. Is tongues required?
Does it really matter? What about the Ethiopian eunuch (Acts 8:27-
39).

Mark 16:15-16 (KJV)

*And he said unto them, Go ye into all the world, and preach
the gospel to every creature. He that believeth and is
baptized shall be saved; but he that believeth not shall be
damned.*

Mark's version of the Great Commission gives us another
insight. It takes belief and baptism to be saved, but only non-belief to
be damned, condemned. So how would the thief on the cross or the
folks from the Old Testament qualify? Let's ask an even tougher
question, "Which Baptism?" The baptism of John, the baptism of the
Holy Spirit, the baptism in water. Before you answer think about the
folks that truly believe you are not baptized unless you are baptized
in the Jordan River. Does it matter?

Matthew 20:21-24 (KJV)

*And he said unto her, What wilt thou? She saith unto him,
Grant that these my two sons may sit, the one on thy right*

hand, and the other on the left, in thy kingdom. But Jesus answered and said, Ye know not what ye ask. Are ye able to drink of the cup that I shall drink of, and to be baptized with the baptism that I am baptized with? They say unto him, We are able. And he saith unto them, Ye shall drink indeed of my cup, and be baptized with the baptism that I am baptized with: but to sit on my right hand, and on my left, is not mine to give, but it shall be given to them for whom it is prepared of my Father. And when the ten heard it, they were moved with indignation against the two brethren.

Jesus uses baptism here in a strange way if we are only talking about immersion in water. It sounds like he is using the word to mean immersed or dyed or even troubles. He is definitely not talking about being submerged in water; he is talking of being submerged in the plan, purpose, or results of Jesus' life. One of those brothers died for Christ as a martyr and the other lived in persecution for Christ. The word baptism here is the same Greek word as the baptism in the passages referenced above.

I will not give you an answer as to the meaning of Baptism; instead I will allow you to make up your own mind at the leading of the Holy Spirit. I picked on Baptism because it is an easy Doctrine with which to challenge you. With all the passages and 'what ifs' we just looked at, can you see how so many interpretations can be made on just that one simple point of faith?

I will leave the other doctrines for you to examine in the same light of the Word.

1 Corinthians 3:3-4 (ESV)

For you are still of the flesh. For while there is jealousy and strife among you, are you not of the flesh and behaving only in a human way? For when one says, "I follow Paul," and another, "I follow Apollos," are you not being merely human?

The Holy Spirit leading Paul writes that division is an outcome of being unsaved, in the flesh, jealous, envying, proud, and merely human. To be only in the flesh is to be unsaved, that is to be without the reconciliation brought about by faith in Christ. In verses 1 and 2 of this passage, this church is told they are acting like little children.

What do little children act like? They are selfish, self-serving, demanding of their own way, choosing up sides in competition, friends one minute and enemies the next, and just plain immature in all things. The results of this are also brought out in:

1 Corinthians 11:17-19 (ESV)

But in the following instructions I do not commend you, because when you come together it is not for the better but for the worse. For, in the first place, when you come together as a church, I hear that there are divisions among you. And I believe it in part, for there must be factions among you in order that those who are genuine among you may be recognized.

Divisions and factions, schisms, are condemned by the Word. They are wrong, totally wrong. It is interesting that in this passage Paul says they are necessary, but for what? Read it carefully. Factions are needed so that the true believers will be made known.

How does that happen?

If we all were led, truly led, by the Holy Spirit and never allowed ourselves to get in the way, there would be no divisions. In a perfect congregation there would be no divisions. Ephesians 4:1-16 says that our growth, maturity will bring us to oneness, UNITY, because of, in, the Holy Spirit. The relevant verses are:

Ephesians 4:1-16 (ESV)

> *I therefore, a prisoner for the Lord, urge you to walk in a manner worthy of the calling to which you have been called, with all humility and gentleness, with patience, bearing with one another in love, eager to maintain the unity of the Spirit in the bond of peace. There is one body and one Spirit—just as you were called to the one hope that belongs to your call— one Lord, one faith, one baptism, one God and Father of all, who is over all and through all and in all. But grace was given to each one of us according to the measure of Christ's gift.*
>
> *Therefore it says, "When he ascended on high he led a host of captives, and he gave gifts to men." (In saying, "He ascended," what does it mean but that he had also descended into the lower regions, the earth? He who descended is the one who also ascended far above all the heavens, that he might fill all things.) And he gave the apostles, the prophets, the evangelists, the shepherds and teachers, to equip the saints for the work of ministry, for building up the body of Christ,* ***until we all attain to the unity of the faith and of the***

knowledge of the Son of God, to mature manhood, to the measure of the stature of the fullness of Christ, so that we may no longer be children, tossed to and fro by the waves and carried about by every wind of doctrine, by human cunning, by craftiness in deceitful schemes. Rather, speaking the truth in love, we are to grow up in every way into him who is the head, into Christ, from whom the whole body, joined and held together by every joint with which it is equipped, when each part is working properly, makes the body grow so that it builds itself up in love.

Do you see it there in **verse 13**? If we were all truly in tune with gifted teachers who are in tune with the Holy Spirit, we will have UNITY of the faith, Unity of knowledge, be mature, and measure up to Christ. Is that going to happen here on earth? All it takes is the change of one word in a statement and there is a different meaning, division.

Therefore, divisions are caused by different understandings of the Word, different teachings of the Word, and different responses to it all. One says this and one says that, if you allow the false understanding or teaching to fester into a division, you are doing what this passage says about being swayed by every wind of human ideas and lying schemes. Since that is fact, you are found to be false and rejected by the true believers. If you don't know what is right and what is wrong, take it to the author of the Word, keeping it to yourself until you learn more.

A caution here. Examine your teachers, preachers, and authors carefully. If what they are saying in any way conflicts with the

Word, call them on it in private. If they will not change or correct their teaching, go to them with 2 or 3 witnesses. If that doesn't work, bring them before the congregation, being well prepared to defend the truth. Why would we carry out Matthew 18:15-16 in this manner? Nothing should offend us more and faster than the misrepresentation of the Word of God. If errors are caught when they happen, they do not become big dividers in the Church. If allowed to fester over time, they will split it once again into factions, which is error in itself.

Question even what I say here. I am not perfect.

As a teacher, I make mistakes. If someone points it out to me, in love, I am more than happy to do whatever it takes to verify my position and then bring it to all to hear. If my position is wrong, I publically recant my statement and reteach the subject. Many times it is a matter of vocabulary and not doctrine.

The ones that do not take part in false teaching and follow the leading of the Word (the instructions Paul talks of in this passage) are the true believers, while the ones who cause and hold to those false teaching divisions are in error and need to be corrected or cast out.

This is difficult to do. It is heart wrenching and spiritually painful. Remember what Jesus taught about the wheat and the tares, and the sheep and the goats, only He can tell the difference. Some that call out, "Lord, Lord," the loudest will be sent away into outer darkness.

Be careful you don't join them.

This shows us that only two divisions are allowed anywhere, those that are God's and those who are not. The Body of Christ is made up of God's. The Church is made up of God's. The church is made up of both.

God's and not God's

Saints and Ain'ts

Imitation or Genuine

How do we know the difference? Paul writing at the leading of the Holy Spirit states that we need divisions because it separates the sheep from the goats (Matthew 25:31-46). How does it do that? Read on in 1 Corinthians 11. Love and the concern/compassion of the Genuines will stand out.

1 Corinthians 12:12-31 (ESV)

> *12 For just as the body is one and has many members, and all the members of the body, though many, are one body, so it is with Christ.*
>
> *13 For in one Spirit we were all baptized into one body—Jews or Greeks, slaves or free—and all were made to drink of one Spirit.*
>
> *14 For the body does not consist of one member but of many.*
>
> *15 If the foot should say, "Because I am not a hand, I do not belong to the body," that would not make it any less a part of the body.*
>
> *16 And if the ear should say, "Because I am not an eye, I do not belong to the body," that would not make it any less a part of the body.*

17 If the whole body were an eye, where would be the sense of hearing? If the whole body were an ear, where would be the sense of smell?

18 But as it is, God arranged the members in the body, each one of them, as he chose.

19 If all were a single member, where would the body be?

20 As it is, there are many parts, yet one body.

21 The eye cannot say to the hand, "I have no need of you," nor again the head to the feet, "I have no need of you."

22 On the contrary, the parts of the body that seem to be weaker are indispensable,

23 and on those parts of the body that we think less honorable we bestow the greater honor, and our unpresentable parts are treated with greater modesty,

24 which our more presentable parts do not require. But God has so composed the body, giving greater honor to the part that lacked it,

25 that there may be no division in the body, but that the members may have the same care for one another.

26 If one member suffers, all suffer together; if one member is honored, all rejoice together.

27 Now you are the body of Christ and individually members of it.

28 And God has appointed in the church first apostles, second prophets, third teachers, then miracles, then gifts of healing, helping, administrating, and various kinds of tongues.

29 Are all apostles? Are all prophets? Are all teachers? Do all work miracles?

30 Do all possess gifts of healing? Do all speak with tongues? Do all interpret?

31 But earnestly desire the higher gifts.

   ✓ The Church is one body.

   ✓ It has many members.

   ✓ In order to do the job it is called to do.

   ✓ The prominent have their honor.

   ✓ The lowly/humble have more honor.

   ✓ The total cannot be divided.

   ✓ The whole body will rejoice or be sad together.

   ✓ Every part has its own role/calling.

The Church is the Body of Christ and, therefore, point blank, must work together, in concert, in order to fulfill its purpose in the world. Could that be the reason the church in America is so ineffective? You cannot chop up a body and expect total functionality. Just take a look at the Wounded Warriors of America today. The condition of the physical body has been damaged to some level. Many of them are able to overcome their partial division, but even the hardest working members of that group still have some restrictions involved in their lives. Even a damaged finger causes disruption in the normal functionality of the human body.

Remember the wheat and tares, sheep and goats? There are body parts that don't belong, but are commonly found: warts, moles, zits, hemorrhoids, etc.

Some members of the church are not a part of the body. The church is that collection of folks who meet in a building a time or two a week. The church is filled with believers and non-believers. Are you confused at this point?

The Church is the Body of Christ. The church is a building where people that are of the Church and those who are not meet. Note the uppercase C and the lowercase c, in that one point Christ's and carnal/earthly/of the flesh are delineated.

Since we have a divisions problem in the church, Paul says we can tell the Church from the church by the signs of a true Believer. How well would you work with an extra arm or two, another foot, more eyes, any extra component parts not connected to the same head and working by different rules? There you are trying to walk to the mail box and the extra two feet want to head out back to take a swim. Counter-productive or what? A battle that would never end. How can the real parts, directed by the head, get anything done, let alone be a strong witness for the head? The Parable of the Sower presents this idea in Mark 4. Lots of seeds to various soils and only the Believers bear fruit because all the parts are in the right place at the right time.

Ephesians 4:1-14 (ESV)

> *1 I therefore, a prisoner for the Lord, urge you to walk in a manner worthy of the calling to which you have been called,*

2 with all humility and gentleness, with patience, bearing with one another in love,

3 eager to maintain the unity of the Spirit in the bond of peace.

4 There is one body and one Spirit—just as you were called to the one hope that belongs to your call—

5 one Lord, one faith, one baptism,

6 one God and Father of all, who is over all and through all and in all.

7 But grace was given to each one of us according to the measure of Christ's gift.

8 Therefore it says, "When he ascended on high he led a host of captives, and he gave gifts to men."

9 (In saying, "He ascended," what does it mean but that he had also descended into the lower regions, the earth?

10 He who descended is the one who also ascended far above all the heavens, that he might fill all things.)

11 And he gave the apostles, the prophets, the evangelists, the shepherds and teachers,

12 to equip the saints for the work of ministry, for building up the body of Christ,

13 until we all attain to the unity of the faith and of the knowledge of the Son of God, to mature manhood, to the measure of the stature of the fullness of Christ,

14 so that we may no longer be children, tossed to and fro by the waves and carried about by every wind of doctrine, by human cunning, by craftiness in deceitful schemes.

Read this passage carefully, again. We looked at it once before. It's important to this entire discussion that you not only read it, but search it in every way you know how.

Paul says he is a prisoner of the Lord, a bond slave.

That is what God called him to be.

In another greeting he has stated that he is a bond slave at the will of the Lord. Then he tells us to live as we are called to live for what reason? Verse 3 says it very simply so that I and hopefully you will be able to understand. *'Eager to maintain the UNITY of the Spirit in the bond of peace.'* We are called to live in humility and gentleness, with patience, lifting up one another in love solely to promote UNITY in the Body of Christ.

In verse 12, the Holy Spirit through the words of Paul tells us that all the gifts, ALL THE GIFTS, are to build us all into the UNITY of the Faith until we are one body in order to grow the Body of Christ in the Knowledge of the Lord and to His stature. In other words, all those gifts are there for our benefit, enabling His people to do the work before them and to grow to be like, to imitate, Christ in all things. UNITY equates with maturity in this passage.

The very gifts we argue over are the gifts that God wants for us to embrace in order to minister in His Name and grow the Body of Christ.

The UNITY God wants is shown by God in:
✓ One body

✓ One Spirit

✓ One hope

✓ One Lord

✓ One faith

✓ One baptism

✓ One God and Father Who is over, through, and in all

Can you see the UNITY involved here? Take any one of these factors out and you have a social club, at best. In today's church environment in America, you have an EASY BELIEVISM, an INDUSTRIAL MODEL OF GRACE, and a totally wasted life.

Even the gifts of the Holy Spirit are for the building up of the Body of Christ into one Body, UNITY. The gifts are to build UNITY and not division.

One thing that UNITY isn't, it is not universalism. Christ is the only way to God. You can't get there through any other way. Not through Allah. Not through Buddha. Not through Krishna. No other way but Jesus.

Ephesians 2:11-22 (ESV)

11 Therefore remember that at one time you Gentiles in the flesh, called "the uncircumcision" by what is called the circumcision, which is made in the flesh by hands—

12 remember that you were at that time separated from Christ, alienated from the commonwealth of Israel and strangers to the covenants of promise, having no hope and without God in the world.

13 But now in Christ Jesus you who once were far off have been brought near by the blood of Christ.

14 For he himself is our peace, who has made us both one and has broken down in his flesh the dividing wall of hostility

15 by abolishing the law of commandments expressed in ordinances, that he might create in himself one new man in place of the two, so making peace,

16 and might reconcile us both to God in one body through the cross, thereby killing the hostility.

17 And he came and preached peace to you who were far off and peace to those who were near.

18 For through him we both have access in one Spirit to the Father.

19 So then you are no longer strangers and aliens, but you are fellow citizens with the saints and members of the household of God,

20 built on the foundation of the apostles and prophets, Christ Jesus himself being the cornerstone,

21 in whom the whole structure, being joined together, grows into a holy temple in the Lord.

22 In him you also are being built together into a dwelling place for God by the Spirit.

Do you see the oneness in this passage?

Believers become citizens of the household of God, one household, and a stone in the holy temple of the Lord. Oneness, UNITY. One Father means one rule maker, one gift giver, one home, one temple, one dwelling place, one body, UNITY. Again, only in Christ.

He has broken down the wall between the Jew and the Gentile in order to make UNITY possible. The wall was man made by the Jews themselves. They had been given the task of showing the world what God could do in the lives of a people, instead they isolated themselves and struggled with God and His precepts to the point God withdrew His protection on many occasions, restoring it always in a way that should have awakened the desire for God. If it was restored, it didn't last long because the people kept coming to the point of naming themselves as the ones in control.

How do we do this? Peter wrote it most simply.

1 Peter 2:1-12 (ESV)

1 So put away all malice and all deceit and hypocrisy and envy and all slander.

2 Like newborn infants, long for the pure spiritual milk, that by it you may grow up into salvation—

3 if indeed you have tasted that the Lord is good.

4 As you come to him, a living stone rejected by men but in the sight of God chosen and precious,

5 you yourselves like living stones are being built up as a spiritual house, to be a holy priesthood, to offer spiritual sacrifices acceptable to God through Jesus Christ.

6 For it stands in Scripture: "Behold, I am laying in Zion a stone, a cornerstone chosen and precious, and whoever believes in him will not be put to shame."

7 So the honor is for you who believe, but for those who do not believe, "The stone that the builders rejected has become the cornerstone,"

8 and "A stone of stumbling, and a rock of offense."

9 But you are a chosen race, a royal priesthood, a holy nation, a people for his own possession, that you may proclaim the excellencies of him who called you out of darkness into his marvelous light.

10 Once you were not a people, but now you are God's people; once you had not received mercy, but now you have received mercy.

11 Beloved, I urge you as sojourners and exiles to abstain from the passions of the flesh, which wage war against your soul.

12 Keep your conduct among the Gentiles honorable, so that when they speak against you as evildoers, they may see your good deeds and glorify God on the day of visitation.

13 Be subject for the Lord's sake to every human institution, whether it be to the emperor as supreme,

Come to the one and only Christ. Get rid of everything that isn't Christ. It all belongs to Him anyhow, acknowledge His ownership and be on the side of the One who saved you. Become a member of a chosen race, a royal priesthood, a holy nation, and a person belonging only to God, for what purpose, to proclaim how wonderful our God is. We were once nobodies and now we are somebodies because we have received mercy available for everybody.

Remember the rich young ruler? He had done all he was supposed to do to have eternal life, but his goods were in the way. He idolized them. Jesus said, "Go and sell all that you have and give it to the poor." In Luke He says, "If you would follow me, die daily, take up your cross and follow me." To be dead is to have nothing, not even life. But, in following we have eternal life and life more abundantly – not in riches, but in what really matters.

Ephesians 2:1-16 (ESV)

1 And you were dead in the trespasses and sins

2 in which you once walked, following the course of this world, following the prince of the power on the air, the spirit that is now at work in the sons of disobedience—

3 among whom we all once lived in the passions of our flesh, carrying out the desires of the body and the mind, and were by nature children of wrath, like the rest of mankind.

4 But God, being rich in mercy, because of the great love with which he loved us,

5 even when we were dead in our trespasses, made us alive together with Christ—by grace you have been saved—

6 and raised us up with him and seated us with him in the heavenly places in Christ Jesus,

7 so that in the coming ages he might show the immeasurable riches of his grace in kindness toward us in Christ Jesus.

8 For by grace you have been saved through faith. And this is not your own doing; it is the gift of God,

9 not a result of works, so that no one may boast.

10 For we are his workmanship, created in Christ Jesus for good works, which God prepared beforehand, that we should walk in them.

11 Therefore remember that at one time you Gentiles in the flesh, called "the uncircumcision" by what is called the circumcision, which is made in the flesh by hands—

12 remember that you were at that time separated from Christ, alienated from the commonwealth of Israel and strangers to the covenants of promise, having no hope and without God in the world.

13 But now in Christ Jesus you who once were far off have been brought near by the blood of Christ.

14 For he himself is our peace, who has made us both one and has broken down in his flesh the dividing wall of hostility

15 by abolishing the law of commandments expressed in ordinances, that he might create in himself one new man in place of the two, so making peace,

16 and might reconcile us both to God in one body through the cross, thereby killing the hostility.

We are saved from the consequences of our sins by one thing, Grace. We have only one pathway, Faith. There is only one Blood that saves, Christ's. There is only one Peace, Christ. There is only one new man, the believer. Hostility, divisions which cause fights, is killed, dead, demolished because there is no difference there is only one body, HIS.

Romans 12:1-2 (ESV)

1 I appeal to you therefore, brothers, by the mercies of God, to present your bodies as a living sacrifice, holy and acceptable to God, which is your spiritual worship.

2 Do not be conformed to this world, but be transformed by the renewal of your mind, that by testing you may discern what is the will of God, what is good and acceptable and perfect.

If there is only one body, HIS, what value is ours? It has no value of itself except to be a living sacrifice to Christ and that is only made real when we conform only to Christ and not to the world. One focus for worship and using your gift of discernment to understand what God wants of you. UNITY, UNITY to continue the work of Christ on the face of the earth. What we believe in, we proclaim to our neighbors, we bet on it, we cheer it, we buy the shirt, chew the gum, and most of all, we argue its superiority with anyone who does not believe that our belief is correct.

Romans 12:18 (ESV)

if possible, so far as it depends on you, live peaceably with all.

UNITY. Not even causing divisions in this world, as much as is possible. Blessed are the peacemakers for they shall be called the children of God. Matthew 5:9. There are times when because of conflict with God's ideals we must raise a ruckus.

Romans 16:17-20 (ESV)

> *17 I appeal to you, brothers, to watch out for those who cause divisions and create obstacles contrary to the doctrine that you have been taught; avoid them.*
>
> *18 For such persons do not serve our Lord Christ, but their own appetites, and by smooth talk and flattery they deceive the hearts of the naive.*
>
> *19 For your obedience is known to all, so that I rejoice over you, but I want you to be wise as to what is good and innocent as to what is evil.*
>
> *20 The God of peace will soon crush Satan under your feet. The grace of our Lord Jesus Christ be with you.*

Those who cause divisions contrary to the Word are to be avoided, do not serve the Body, and deceive the hearts of the lost. The Pharisees were a prime example of this. They knew the Word and added to it all their laws. In adding the extras to the Word, they began contrary and heretical congregations of folks claiming to be the only ones walking the correct path, when in fact they were further from the true path than the blatant sinners.

Then they demanded that everyone follow their practices, deceiving many because of their position and fleshly holiness, if there is such a thing. The one true path is obscured with all their added trash so that no one can find the True Path. Their millstone will carry them deep. They were deceivers and not connected to the Body of Christ. Many of our prominent 'Teachers of the Word' are the new Pharisees. Unfortunately, many called Pastor or Elder in our churches today have joined into that group, basing much of their teaching on additions to the Word, or only teaching portions of the Word that satisfy their additions.

1 Peter 4:1-2 (ESV)

1 Since therefore Christ suffered in the flesh, arm yourselves with the same way of thinking, for whoever has suffered in the flesh has ceased from sin,

2 so as to live for the rest of the time in the flesh no longer for human passions but for the will of God.

Our UNITY is even to be in the way we think. If we didn't get in the way of the Holy Spirit teaching us the truth, we would all come to the same interpretation of Scripture. It is only because we are not UNIFIED with thinking of Christ that we argue and fret with one another all the time.

Philippians 2:1-11 (ESV)

1 So if there is any encouragement in Christ, any comfort from love, any participation in the Spirit, any affection and sympathy,

2 complete my joy by being of the same mind, having the same love, being in full accord and of one mind.

3 Do nothing from selfish ambition or conceit, but in humility count others more significant than yourselves.

4 Let each of you look not only to his own interests, but also to the interests of others.

5 Have this mind among yourselves, which is yours in Christ Jesus,

6 who, though he was in the form of God, did not count equality with God a thing to be grasped,

7 but emptied himself, by taking the form of a servant, being born in the likeness of men.

8 And being found in human form, he humbled himself by becoming obedient to the point of death, even death on a cross.

9 Therefore God has highly exalted him and bestowed on him the name that is above every name,

10 so that at the name of Jesus every knee should bow, in heaven and on earth and under the earth,

11 and every tongue confess that Jesus Christ is Lord, to the glory of God the Father.

How do we accomplish this UNITY of thinking? We accomplish UNITY by being of the same mind, having the same love, being in full accord and of one mind. Emptied of self, by taking the form of a servant, being born in the likeness of men like Christ, and being found in human form, he humbled himself by becoming obedient to the point of death, even death on a cross.

We are told to take up our cross daily. This passage defines what that means. We are to die daily to self and live for Him who died for us.

John 17:20-26 (ESV)

20 "I do not ask for these only, but also for those who will believe in me through their word,

21 that they may all be one, just as you, Father, are in me, and I in you, that they also may be in us, so that the world may believe that you have sent me.

22 The glory that you have given me I have given to them, that they may be one even as we are one,

23 I in them and you in me, that they may become perfectly one, so that the world may know that you sent me and loved them even as you loved me.

24 Father, I desire that they also, whom you have given me, may be with me where I am, to see my glory that you have given me because you loved me before the foundation of the world.

25 O righteous Father, even though the world does not know you, I know you, and these know that you have sent me.

26 I made known to them your name, and I will continue to make it known, that the love with which you have loved me may be in them, and I in them."

Three unities described above:

1. With the Godhead

2. With the Body of Christ – the Church

3. With each other

Matthew 22:34-40 (ESV)

34 But when the Pharisees heard that he had silenced the Sadducees, they gathered together.

35 And one of them, a lawyer, asked him a question to test him.

36 "Teacher, which is the great commandment in the Law?"

37 And he said to him, "You shall love the Lord your God with all your heart and with all your soul and with all your mind.

38 This is the great and first commandment.

39 And a second is like it: You shall love your neighbor as yourself.

40 On these two commandments depend all the Law and the Prophets."

If you read the Word with your focus on UNITY, you will find that the entirety of the Word speaks to UNITY from *"In the beginning God,"* to *"The Grace of our Lord Jesus Christ be with you all, Amen."*

Denominations have done more to harm the Church than any other factor I can think of. More than music, tongues, miracles, sign gifts, sinful pastors, deacons wives, carpet in the nursery, color of the drapes, baptism, anything. That's a big hurt. Think with me for a while in prayerful contemplation.

The Church cannot be destroyed from the outside, so Satan must attack on the inside. There was a famous radio "Bible" teacher holding a three day conference for his audience. The focus of that conference was how his teaching, shared by all the attendees would change the rest of the Body of Christ's thinking to agree with him. His teaching is just as controversial as the other side's teaching. Is one of them wrong? Yes. Does it matter? I don't think so. Both teachings can be Biblically taught and argued. So, why waste a three day conference to teach how to fight in the Body, when there are millions that haven't heard either side and are going to Hell?

The polls indicate that 70% or more of the folks in these United States claim to be Christian. That's a voting block of 80% of the voters. Why don't the candidates play to Christians? They play to the NRA at only 5% of the population. They play to the blacks at only 14% of the population. They play to women at 51% of the population. They play to Hispanics 18%, LGBT 3%, farmers, unions, and every other small group around, but not to Christians.

Could it be that our division into denominations is causing this? The answer is yes.

We, the Body of Christ, spend so much time selling our denomination, we don't proclaim Christ, and instead, we proclaim our denomination. How many churches, campuses of buildings, are there in your community? Do they work together other than the annual Easter Sun Rise service, maybe? Does the conversation between the churches extend beyond the pastors maybe having breakfast together once a month or so?

I can remember when the pastors of the denomination where I was called to pastor, told me that unless I was baptized in a XXXXX church, I would not go to heaven. Only XXXXX denomination was going to heaven. What a lie? And, they believed it. That was only 25 years ago.

Isn't that a sad proclamation?

That is not Biblical. There are only three denominations listed in Scripture. They are Church of God, Church of Christ, and Baptist. The last one is a stretch. This paragraph is a joke in case you need to be told.

No, I am not advocating the dissolution of the denominations, nor am I advocating the restoration of the one world church. (It will come on its own in the end times. I probably should not say that because we all disagree on Eschatology so much I could start a fight.)

What Christ the Word and I are advocating is for all of us to become THE BODY OF CHRIST. Would it matter to any of us who was the fingernail, or who got the role of tongue, as long as the Lord is the head? If it did, those would be the folks to ignore and move on.

If you want a solemn robed service, go for it. If you want rock and roll music, go for it. If you want to dance in the aisles, do it. If you prefer to kneel and pray, go for that, too. I don't care what the name is over the door and neither does Christ, but He cares what is being done with the Grace of God and His Word.

We are not told to preach our interpretation, we are told to preach the Word. We are not told to go to church, we are told to be the Church. We are not told to say a sinner's prayer and all is well. We are told to surrender to a Holy God thru faith in Christ.

The Church is to be UNITED outside walls in the middle of communities all over the world showing Christ to those who don't know him. Just think of the workforce that would be present in your community if the churches united into The Church for the benefit of all in Christ. Not all into one big church, but united in purpose and love and intent and mission.

UNITY is the key to the Power of a Holy God. All of us can be much more than one of us can be.

Because this issue is so important, at the end of 1st Corinthians, Paul says in 16:17, *"Now I beseech you, brethren, mark them which cause divisions and offences contrary to the doctrine which ye have learned; and avoid them."*

Personal Evangelism

Witnessing (Personal Evangelism) is a commandment.
Matthew 28:18-20 ESV

> *And Jesus came and said to them, "All authority in heaven and on earth has been given to me. Go therefore and make disciples of all nations, baptizing them in the name of the Father and of the Son and of the Holy Spirit, teaching them to observe all that I have commanded you. And behold, I am with you always, to the end of the age."*

Acts 26:16 KJV

> *But rise, and stand upon thy feet: for I have appeared unto thee for this purpose, to make thee a minister and a witness both of these things which though hast seen, and of those things in which I will reveal unto thee:*

What is personal evangelism? It is simply defined as witnessing and providing discipleship.

Witnessing is defined as "showing through your life and words that Jesus Christ is Lord of your life."

Discipleship is defined as "leading another to the Lordship of Jesus Christ in their life."

Those are very simplistic definitions, but they will serve for now.

The Great Commission (Matthew 28:18-20, Mark 16:15-18, John 21:15-17, Acts 1:3-8) commands us to make disciples of all nations, baptizing them in the name of the Father, the Son, and the Holy Spirit. In order to make disciples, you must be a witness. In order to be a witness, you must have received God's salvation.

God doesn't give us any command that HE does not give us the power to accomplish.

Acts 1:8 KJV
> But ye shall receive power, after that the Holy Ghost is come upon you: and ye shall be witnesses unto me both in Jerusalem, and in all Judea, and in Samaria, and unto the uttermost part of the earth.

Witnessing comes in two catagories.
1. To the unsaved
2. To the saved - admonishing and discipleship.

2 Timothy 2:1-2 KJV
> *Thou therefore, my son, be strong in the grace that is in Christ Jesus. And the things that thou hast heard of me*

among many witnesses, the same commit thou to faithful men, who shall be able to teach others also.

Three types of witnessing
1. Assignment - meet with a certain person
2. Natural - when we meet them in life
3. Specialized - aimed at a culture or group

The key to witnessing is RELATIONSHIPS. Sometimes you must earn your right to share what you believe. It could take a long time, years even, or a short meet up, like sitting next to someone on a plane.

Think of all the horrible, no good things that have ever happened to you.

Think of all the great, wonderful, fantastic things that have happened to you.

The answer to the bad days most likely dealt with broken relationships.
The answer to the good days probably dealt with fulfilled relationships.

There are two types of relationships

1. Vertical- to God

2. Horizontal- to man

Neither can be complete without the other. Draw a line representing the two types of relationships and you have the cross.

Amos 3:3 asks
Can two walk together except they be agreed?

Our vertical relationship must be right before we can hold up our horizontal relationships. For we are only able to meet another's needs from God's provision, never from our own efforts.

Matthew 19:19 tells us to love our neighbor as ourselves - If we do not have God's love in us, we don't truly love ourselves enough to love others.

The scary part of this is forgiving. We must be forgiven and we must forgive. How else can we love each other enough to carry out the commandment of going to all corners of the earth? How else can we love enough to share the Good News that has made us new.

Matthew 6:14-15 explains the only part of the Lord's prayer that is explained. We must forgive that we might be forgiven. The hardest command of them all, we must forgive ourselves.

First we get ourselves right with God.
Rom 12:1-2
Ps 51:10-13,

2 Cor. 5:18-20

The reason for not witnessing is FEAR.
2 Tim 1:7
John 15:5
1 Cor. 2

Go to God about the person before you go to the person about God. In other words, pray for them before you talk to them, or even pray to meet someone, anyone before you start your day.

Specific persons - pray specifically for the individual before you take the Gospel, the Good News to someone.

The unknown man - pray to be alert to opportunities to be used when the present themselves.

Pray in specifics
People by name
Needs if known
Expectations Desires
To be used and how.

The approach

Lifestyle witnessing

✓ Your life is a witness for Christ.

✓ Your life is guided by the Holy Spirit.

✓ You are to be bold in the Spirit Acts 4:13, 2 Cor. 3:12

✓ You speak from overflow not filling. Acts 4:20

✓ Your life glorifies God. 1 Cor. 1:31,10:31

How to go about it

✓ Be a listener

✓ Be a friend

✓ Don't exclude, include; after all it is God's bounty

✓ Pray

✓ Study to show thyself approved, rightly dividingThe Word of Truth.

✓ Be there in times of joy and trouble

The cults grow because they are meeting needs, real needs, and perceived needs, in the lives of people, how can we do anything else?

The message: sample from Acts 22:1-16, 1 Cor. 14:9

Your testimony is entitled - My life before receiving Christ

Romans 3:23

Romans 6:23a

How I realized I needed Christ

Cor. 2:2

Cor. 2:17

Matt 16:26

Romans 6:23b

Remember those memories of the horrible, no good, very bad, terrible days we talked of earlier? How did you feel then? What made the change in your life? What has God done for you in relationships? How have you been blessed on a general basis? Folks want to know that our God Reigns and the Reigns well.

How I became a Christian –

Gal 2:20

John 3:16-17

Romans 10:13

How Christ helped me in my life today –

2 Cor. 3:12

Remember:

✓ Your testimony is important, you are God's person.

✓ Be prepared

✓ Keep it short and simple

✓ Keep your testimony to the point

✓ Adequate details are important

✓ Avoid bragging and negative remarks

✓ Don't compare religions

✓ Don't denigrate (put down) their religion

✓ Don't use church words without explaining them

Using Scripture:

✓ Use it this way

✓ You do the reading

✓ Let them look on

✓ Don't hurry

✓ Just read, don't stop and preach

✓ Watch for interest, if none, stop

✓ If no interest, ask if it's making sense

✓ Be sensitive to needs and questions

✓ Ask for a response to the Word

Don't get too excited about the order, or content, or how to pronounce it, God will provide.

Relax and be natural.

Topics

What follows are short outlines on various topics.

They can be used for personal devotions,

group lessons,

sermons,

or whatever you would like.

Salvation

Sin came into this world - Romans 5:12

The penalty for sin - Romans 6:23

All are sinners - Romans 3:21-26   The penalty paid

The Gift - Romans 5:15-21, Ephesians 2:4-10, Romans 10:17, Galatians 23:16

Why Jesus? John 3:16-17 Romans 1:16

What He did - Colossians 1:21-2, 23:1-4

How to get the gift - Romans 10:9-13

ATTITUDE

Attitude of those searching for God - Matthew 18:1-14

BIBLE

Given - II peter 1:19-21

Given & Use - II Timothy 3:16-17

Purpose - Psalm 119:11, Galatians 1:6-9

Eternality - Matthew 5:17-18

Lack of Knowledge is Error - Matthew 22:29

CARNAL MINDNESS

Conflicts with the inner man. - Romans 7:14-22

Conflicts with the Holy Spirit - Galatians 5:17

Enmity with God - Romans 8:6-8, James 4:4

In the children of Wrath - Ephesians 2:3

Is to be Crucified - Romans 8:13, Galatians 5:24

Excludes from kingdom of God Galatians - 5:19-21

Reaps corruption - Galatians 6:8

CHURCH

Cornerstone and members - 1 Peter 2:5-10

Purpose - Hebrews 10:24-25, Romans 15:1-7

Government - Acts 6:1-4

DOUG BALL

COMMUNION

Instituted - Matthew 26:26-29, Mark 14:22-25, Luke 22:17-20

Abuses - 1 Corinthians 11:20-31

Importance - John 6:53-64

DEPRESSION

John 3:16-17

Lamentations 3:21-27

Hebrews 4:12-16

James 5:14-16

Ecclesiastes 4:9-12

Genesis 4:6-7

Philippians 4:4-13

Psalm 118:23-24

Ephesians 3:20-21

Hebrews 12:1-3 1

Peter 5:6-10

Joshua 1:8-9

We change by working against self and toward/for Christ.

FAITH

Defined:

Hebrews 11:1

Read all of chapter 11 for examples.
This is called the "Faith" chapter.

2 Corinthians 4:18
Why Faith?

2 Corinthians 5:7
Our Christian walk.

Romans 1:17
Faith grows from faith.

The just shall live by faith.

GOD

One God in three persons

The term "Trinity" is not found in the Bible. It is a term we use to denote the Father, Son, and the Holy Spirit as God, the one and only God.

The Bible doesn't offer explanations of HOW three can be one. The Bible just makes the statement of the fact and makes no attempt to defend it. God needs no defense. The Bible tells us that:

- ✓ God the Father is God.
- ✓ Jesus, God the son, is God.
- ✓ The Holy Spirit is God.

HOW MANY GODS ARE THERE?

Isaiah 43:10-15

Vs 11-God is THE Savior

Vs 13 No one can control God

Vs 15-Your King Isaiah 44:6-8

Vs 6- Beside me there is no God

Vs 8-1 know not any. (and God knows all) Isaiah 45:12,18,& 22

Vs 12- The Creator, the only one

Vs 18- There is none else

Vs 22- There is none else, (by which to be saved) Mark 12:29-31

Vs 29- The Lord our God is one Lord:

Vs 30- The first law

THERE IS ONLY ONE CREATOR, ONE GOD, ONE LORD, ONE SAVIOR.

WHO IS JESUS?

John 1:1-3, 14

Vs 1- The WORD was GOD

Vs 3- The WORD was the creator

Vs 14- The WORD became man

Genesis 1:1-3

Vs 1- In the beginning God...

Vs 2- The Spirit of God

Vs 3- Let there be light

Colossians 1:15-18

Vs 15- the image of God

Vs 16-The creator who things were created for

Vs 17-He holds everything together

Vs 18- The head of the church John 10:30-33

Vs 30-1 and my Father are one

Vs 31- Why stone him?

Vs 33- Makest thyself God

John 10:38- Father is in me and I in Him

John 17:11- They may be one, as we are

John 17:21-23- Even as we are one

John 20:27-29- My Lord and my God

WHO ONLY IS TO BE WORSHIPED AND SERVED?

Exodus 20:1-6

Vs 2-1 am God

Vs 3- Thou shalt have no other gods before me Vs 4- No idols

Vs 5- Serve (worship) only God

Acts 14:8-15- Worship only god no matter what a man does

Matthew 4:9-10- Thou shalt worship the Lord thy God, and Him only shalt thou serve.

Hebrews 1:6-And let all the angels of God worship Him.

Matthew 2:2- Come to worship Him.

Matthew 2:8- That I may come and worship Him also.

Matthew 2:11- fell down and worshiped Him.

John 9:38- he worshiped Him.

Philippians 2:9-10- every knee shall bow.

Isaiah 45:23- to me every knee shall bow.

Romans 14:10-12- every knee shall bow.

WHO DOES THE FATHER SAY JESUS IS?

Hebrews 1:8- Thy throne, O God, is for ever and ever.

WHO IS THE SAVIOR?

Titus 1:3-4

Vs 3- God our Savior.

Vs 4- Lord Jesus Christ our Savior.

Titus 3:4,6

Vs 4- God our Savior.

Vs 6- Jesus Christ our Savior.

Psalm 27:1

Vs 1- God is light and salvation. Psalm 62:1

Vs 1- God is my salvation.

Jude 25- God is Savior.

WHO IS THE HOLY SPIRIT?

Genesis 1:2 - The Spirit of God .

Romans 8:9 - The Spirit of God dwell in you.

Acts 1:7-8 - God's power giver.

Acts 2:1-4 - Filled with the Holy Ghost.

Acts 5:3-4

Vs 3-Ananias lied to the Holy Spirit.

Vs 4-Ananias lied to God.

CONCLUSION

Romans 8:9-14

Vs 9- We are the Spirit, The spirit of God, The Spirit of Christ.

Vs 10- Christ in you.

Vs 11- The spirit of Him that raised Jesus from the dead. Make your mortal bodies alive by
His Spirit that dwelleth in you.

✓ God the Father is God.

✓ Jesus, God the Son is God.

✓ The Holy Spirit is God.

Special thanks to Steve Coombe for the major part of the research presented here

On Being Fed

Acts 20:28 - Paul's charge to the elders at Ephesus

1 Corinthians 3:1-2 - The food of the masses in the church

Peter 2:1-3 - A desire must be there. IT is man's responsibility

Luke 12:22-40 - What do we seek?

Romans 14 - How to feed.

Matthew 25:31-46 - Judgment Day

MONEY

New testament giving.

Corinthians 9:6-11

Hebrews 13:15

Peter 3:7

Peter 1:5-9

OVERCOMING

Have a reason to go on.

Luke 18:7-8

Psalm 37

Let God's word encourage you.

Hebrews 4:12-13, 11:6

Study the situation and look at the options.

John 10:1-5

James 1:17

Go on the attack.

Phil 4:13

Col 3:12-17

Let Christ walk with you.

Eph 3:14-21

We change by working against ourselves

TITHE

Leviticus 27:30-31 Law

Numbers 18:26-28

Deut. 26:12 & 14:22

All words translated as tithe in the KJV in either Hebrew, Aramaic or Greek mean 1/10, or give, take, paid, collected 1/10.

Genesis 14:20 Abraham gave 1/10 as thanksgiving

Genesis 28:22 Jacob promised 1/10 in thanksgiving

Malachi 3:8 Withholding tithes is stealing from God

Hebrews 7 all of it especially verse 8

2 Corinthians 9

STATEMENT OF FAITH

Most churches and/or denominations have what is called a Statement of Faith or What We Believe. If you are looking for a church that is the first thing you want to check. Not the gym, nursery, or pew padding, but what that congregation believes. What they believe, they will teach? What they believe, they will promulgate. Everything they do will be based on what they believe. The second thing you want to check out is what they do. That will show you what they really believe.

This is a sample of a Statement of Faith.

This happens to be the Statement of Faith of the Southern Baptist Convention. Its placement here is neither an endorsement nor a statement of *if you don't believe this, you are going to hell.* It is purely a sample I have at my fingertips.

Doctrine

Taken from the Baptist Faith and Message @2000 –
Southern Baptist Convention

I THE SCRIPTURES

The Holy Bible was written by men divinely inspired and is God's revelation of Himself to man. It is a perfect treasure of divine instruction. It has God for its author, salvation for its end, and truth, without any mixture of error, for its matter. Therefore, all Scripture is totally true and trustworthy. It reveals the principles by which God judges us, and therefore is, and will remain to the end of the world, the true center of Christian union, and supreme standard by which all human conduct, creeds, and religious opinions should be tried. All Scripture is a testimony to Christ, who is Himself the focus of divine revelation.

Exodus 24:4; Deuteronomy 4:1-2; 17-19; Joshua 8:34; Psalms 19:7-10; 119:11,89,105,140; Isaiah 34:16; 40:8; Jeremiah 15:16; 36:1-32: Matthew 5:17-18: 22:29; Luke 21:33; 24:44-46; John 5:39; 16:13-15; 17:17; Acts2:16ff.; 17:11; Romans 15:4; 16:25-26; 2 Timothy 3:15-17; Hebrews 1:1-2; 4:12; 1 Peter 1:25; 2 Peter 1:19-21.

II GOD

There is one and only one living and true God. He is an intelligent, spiritual, and personal being, the Creator, Redeemer, Preserver, and Ruler of the universe. God is infinite in holiness and all other perfections. God is powerful and all knowing; and His perfect knowledge extends to all things, past, present, and future, including the future decisions of His free creatures. To Him we owe the highest love, reverence, and obedience. The eternal triune God reveals Himself to us as Father, Son, and Holy Spirit, with distinct personal attributes, but without division of nature, essence, or being.

A. God the Father

God the Father reigns with providential care over His universe, His creations, and the flow of the stream of human history according to the purposes of His grace. He is all powerful, all knowing, all loving, and all wise. God is Father in truth to those who become children of God through faith in Jesus Christ. He is fatherly in His attitude toward all men.

Genesis 1:1; 2:7; Exodus 3:14; 6:2-3; 15:11 ff; 20:1 ff.; Leviticus 22:2; Deuteronomy 6:4; 32:6; 1 Chronicles 29:10; Psalm 19:1-3; Isaiah 43:3,15; 64:8; Jeremiah 10:10; 17:13; Matthew 6:9ff; 7:11; 23:9; 28:19; Mark 1:9-11; John 4:24; 5:26; 14:6-13; 17:1-8; Acts 1:7; Romans 8:14-15; 1 Corinthians 8:6; Galatians 4:6; Ephesians

4:6; Colossians 1:15; 1 Timothy 1:17; Hebrews 11:6; 12:9; 1 Peter 1:17: 1 John 5:7

B. God the Son

Christ is the eternal Son of God. In His incarnation as Jesus Christ He was conceived of the Holy Spirit and born of the virgin Mary. Jesus was perfectly revealed and did the will of God, taking upon Himself human nature with its demands and necessities and identifying Himself completely with mankind yet without sin. He honored the divine law by His personal obedience, and in His substitutionary death on the cross He made provision for the redemption of men from sin. He was raised from the dead with a glorified body and appeared to His disciples as the person He was with them before His crucifixion. He ascended into heaven and is now exalted at the right hand of God where He is the One Mediator, fully God, fully man, in whose Person is effected the reconciliation between God and man. He will return in power and glory to judge the world and to consummate His redemptive mission. He now dwells in all believers as the living and ever present Lord.

Genesis 18: 1 ff.; Psalms 2:7 ff.; 110:1 ff.; Isaiah 7:14; 53; Matthew 1:18-3; 3:17; 8:29; 11:27; 14:33; 16:16, 27; 17:5,27; 28:1-6,19; Mark 1:1; 3:11; Luke 1:35; 4:41; 22:70; 24:46; John 1:1-18,29; 10:30,38; 11:25-27; 12:44-50; 14:7-11; 16:15-26,28; 17:1-5, 21-22; 20:1-20,28; Acts 1:9; 2:22-24; 7:55-56; 9:4-5,20; Romans 1:3-4; 3:23-26; 5:6-21; 8:1-3, 34; 10:4; 1 Corinthians 1:30; 2:2; 8:6; 15:1-8, 24-28; 2 Corinthians 5:19-21; 8:9; Galatians 4:4-5; Ephesians 1:20; 3:11; 4:7-10; Philippians 2:5-1 1; Colossians 1:13-22; 2:9; 1

Thessalonians 4:14-18; 1 Timothy 2:5-6; 3:16; Titus 2:13-14; Hebrews 1:1-3; 4: 14-15; 7: 14-28; 9:12-15, 24-28; 12:2 13:8; 1 Peter 2:21-25; 3:22; John 1:7-9; 3:2; 4:14-15; 5:9; 2John 7-9; Revelation 1:13-16; 5:9-14; 12:10-11; 13:8; 19:16.

C. God the Holy Spirit

The Holy Spirit is the Spirit of God, fully divine. He inspired holy men of old to write the Scriptures. Through illumination He enables men to understand truth. He exalts Christ. He convicts men of sin, of righteousness, and of judgment. He calls men to the Savior, and effects regeneration. At the moment of regeneration He baptizes every believer into the Body of Christ. He cultivates Christian character, comforts believers, and bestows the spiritual gifts by which they serve God through His church. He seals the believer unto the day of final redemption. His presence in the Christian guarantees that God will bring the believer into the fullness of the stature of Christ. He enlightens and empowers the believer and the church in worship, evangelism, and service.

Genesis 1:2; Judges 14:6; Job 26:13; Psalms 51:11; 139:7ff; Isaiah 61:1-3; Joel 2:28-32 ; Matthew 1:18; 3:16; 4:1; 12:28-32; 28:19; Mark 1:10,12; Luke 1:35; 4:1,18-19; 11:13; 12:12; 24:49; John 4:24; 14:16-17, 26; 15:26; 16:7-14; Acts 1:8; 2:1-4, 38; 4:31; 5:3; 6:3; 7:55; 8:17, 39; 10:44; 13:2; 15:28; 16:6; 19:1-6; Romans 8:9-11, 14-16, 26-27; 1 Corinthians 2:10-14; 3:16; 12:3-11, 13; Galatians 4:6; Ephesians 1:13-14; 4:30; 5:18; 1 Thessalonians 5:19; 1 Timothy 1:14; 3:16; Hebrews 9:8,14; 2 Peter 1:21; 1 John 4:13; 5:6-7; Revelation 1:10; 22:17.

III MAN

Man is the special creation of God, made in His own image. He created them male and female as the crowning work of his creation. The gift of gender is thus part of the goodness of God's creation. In the beginning man was innocent of sin and was endowed by his Creator with freedom of choice. By his free choice man sinned against God and brought sin into the human race. Through the temptation of Satan man transgressed the command of God, and fell from his original innocence whereby his posterity inherit a nature and an environment inclined toward sin. Therefore, as soon as they are capable of moral action, they become transgressors and are under condemnation. Only the grace of god can bring man into His holy fellowship and enable man to fulfill the creative purpose of god. The sacredness of human personality is evident in that God created man in His own image, and in that Christ died for man; therefore, every person of every race possesses full dignity and is worthy of respect and Christian love.

Genesis 1:26-30; 2:5,7, 18-22; 3; 9:6; Psalms 1; 8:3-6; 32:1-5; 51:5; Isaiah 6:5; Jeremiah 17:5; Matthew 16:26; Acts 17:26-31; Romans 1:19-32; 3:10-18, 23; 5:6, 12,19; 6:6; 7:14-25; 8:14-18, 29; 1 Corinthians 1:21-31; 15:19, 21-22; Ephesians 2:1-22; Colossians 1:21-22; 3:9-11.

IV SALVATION

Salvation involves the redemption of the whole man, and is offered freely to all who accept Jesus Christ as Lord and Savior, who by His own blood obtained eternal redemption for the believer. In its broadest sense salvation includes regeneration, justification, sanctification, and glorification. There is no salvation apart from personal faith in Jesus Christ as Lord.

Regeneration, or the new birth, is a work of God's grace whereby believers become new creatures in Christ Jesus. It is a change of heart wrought by the Holy Spirit through conviction of sin, to which the sinner responds in repentance toward god and faith in the Lord Jesus Christ. Repentance and faith are now inseparable experiences of grace.

Repentance is genuine turning from sin toward God. Faith is acceptance of Jesus Christ and commitment of the entire personality to Him as Lord and Savior.

Justification is God's gracious and full acquittal upon principles of His righteousness of all who repent and believe in Christ. Justification brings the believer unto a relationship of peace and favor with God.

Sanctification is the experience, beginning in regeneration, by which the believer is set apart to God's purposes, and is enabled to progress toward moral and spiritual maturity through the presence and power of the Holy Spirit dwelling in him. Growth in grace should continue throughout the regenerate person's life.

Glorification is the culmination of salvation and is the final blessed and abiding state of the redeemed.

Genesis 3:15; Exodus 3:14-17; 6:2-8; Matthew 1:21; 4:17; 16:21-26; 27:22-28:6; Luke 1:68-69; 2:28-32; John 1:11-14; 29; 3:3-21, 36; 5:24; 10:9, 28-29; 15:1-6; 17:17; Acts 2:21; 4:12; 15:11; 16:30-31; 17:30-31; 20:32; Romans 1:16-18; 2:4; 3:32-35; 4:3 ff.; 5:8-10; 6:1-23; 8:1-18,29-39; 10:9-10, 13; 13:11-14; 1 Corinthians 5:17-20; Galatians 2:20; 3:13; 5:22-25; 6:15; Ephesians 1:7; 2:8-22; 4:11-16; Philippians 2:12-13; Colossians 1:9-22; 3:1 ff.; 1 Thessalonians 5:23-24; 2 Timothy 1:12; Titus 2:11-14; Hebrews 2:1-3; 5:8-9; 9:24-28; 11:1-12:8, 14; James 2:14-26; 1 Peter 1:2-23; 1 John 1:6-2:11; Revelation 3:20; 21:1-22:5.

V ELECTION

Election is the gracious purpose of God, according to which He regenerates, justifies, sanctifies, and glorifies sinners. It is consistent with the free agency of man, and comprehends all the means in the connection with the end. It is the glorious display of God's sovereign goodness, and is infinitely wise, holy, and unchangeable. It excludes boasting and promotes humility.

All true believers endure to the end. Those whom God has accepted in Christ, and sanctified by His Spirit, will never fall away from the state of grace, but shall preserve to the end. Believers may fall into sin through neglect and temptation, whereby they grieve the Spirit, impair their graces and comforts, and bring reproach on the cause of Christ and temporal judgments on themselves; yet they shall be kept by the power of God through faith unto salvation.

Genesis 12:1-3; Exodus 19:5-8; 1 Samuel 8:4-7,19-22; Isaiah 5:1-7; Jeremiah 31:31 ff.; Matthew 16:18-19; 21:28-45; 24:22,31; 25:34; Luke 1:68-79; 2:29-32; 19:41-44; 24:44-48; John 1:12-14; 3:16; 5:24; 6:44-45, 65; 10:27-29; 15:16; 17:6, 12, 17-18; Acts 20-32; Romans 5:9-10; 8:28-39; 10:12-15; 11:5-7, 26-36; 1 Corinthians 1:1-2; 15:24-28; Ephesians 1:4-23; 2:1-10; 3:1-11; Colossians 1:12-14; 2 Thessalonians 2:13-14; 2 Timothy 1:12; 2:10, 19; Hebrews 11:39-12:2; James 1:12; 1 Peter 1:2-5, 13; 2:4-10; 1 John 1:7-9; 2:19; 3:2.

VI THE CHURCH

A new testament church of the Lord Jesus Christ is an autonomous local congregation of baptized believers, associated by covenant in the faith and fellowship of the gospel; observing the two ordinances of Christ, governed by His laws, exercising the gifts, rights, and privileges invested in them by His Word, and seeking to extend the gospel to the ends of the earth. Each congregation operates under the Lordship of Christ through democratic processes. In such a congregation each member is responsible and accountable to Christ as Lord. Its scriptural officers are pastors and deacons. While both men and women are gifted for service in the church, the office of pastor is limited to men as qualified Scripture.

The New Testament speaks also of the church as the Body of Christ which includes all of the redeemed of all the ages, believers from every tribe, and tongue, and people, and nation.

Matthew 16:15-19; 18:15-20; Acts 2:41-42, 47; 5:11-14; 6:3-6; 13:1-3; 14:23,27; 15:1-30; 16:5; 20:28; Romans 1:7; 1 Corinthians 1:2; 3:16; 5:4-5; 7:17; 9:13-14; 12; Ephesians 1:22-23; 2:19-22; 3:8-11, 21; 5:22-32; Philippians 1:1; Colossians 1:18; 1 Timothy 2:9-124; 3:1-15; 4:14; Hebrews 11:39-40; 1 Peter 5:1-4; Revelation-3; 21:2-3.

VII. BAPTISM AND THE LORD'S SUPPER

Christian baptism is the immersion of a believer in water in the name of the Father, the Son, and the Holy Spirit. It is an act of symbolizing the believer's faith in a crucified, buried, and risen Savior, the believer's death to sin, burial of the old life, and resurrection of the dead. Being a church ordinance, it is prerequisite to the privileges of church membership and to the Lord's Supper.

The Lord's Supper is a symbolic act of obedience whereby members of the church, through partaking of the bread and the fruit of the vine, memorialize the death of the Redeemer and anticipate His second coming.

Matthew 3:13-17; 26:26-30; 28:19-20; Mark 1:9-11; 14:22-26; Luke 3:21-22; 22:19-20; John 3:23; Acts 2:41-42; 8:35-39; 16:30-33; 20:7; Romans 6:3-5; 1 Corinthians 10:16,21; 11:23-29; Colossians 2:12.

VIII THE LORD'S DAY

The first day of the week is the Lord's Day. It is a Christian institution for regular observance. It commemorates the resurrection of Christ from the dead and should include exercises of worship and spiritual devotion, both public and private. Activities on the Lord's Day should be commensurate with the Christian's conscience under the Lordship of Jesus Christ.

Exodus 20:8-11; Matthew 12:1-12; 28:1 ff.; Mark 2:27-28; 16:1-7; Luke 24:1-3, 33-36; John 4:21-24; 20:1, 19-28; Acts 20:7; Romans 14:5-10; 1 Corinthians 16:1-2; Colossians 2:16; 3:16; Revelation 1:10.

IX THE KINGDOM

The Kingdom of God includes both His general sovereignty over the universe and His particular kiinship over men who willfully acknowledge Him as King. Particularly the Kingdom is the realm of salvation into which men enter by trustful, childlike commitment to Jesus Christ. Christians ought to pray and to labor that the Kingdom may come and God's will be done on earth. The full consummation of the Kingdom awaits the return of Jesus Christ and the end of this age.

Genesis 1:1; Isaiah 9:6-7; Jeremiah 23:5-6; Matthew 3:2; 4:8-10, 23; 12:25-28; 13:1-52; 25:31-46; 26:29; Mark 1:14-15; 9:1; Luke 4:42; 8:1; 9:2; 12:31-32; 17:20-21; 23:42; John 3:3; 18:36; Acts 1:6-7; 17:22-31; Romans 5:17; 8:19; 1 Corinthians 15:24-28; Colossians 1:13; Hebrews 11:10, 16; 12:28; 1 Peter 2:4-10; 4:13; Revelation 1:6, 9; 5:10; 11:15; 21-22.

X LAST THINGS

God, in His own time and in his own way, will bring the world to its appropriate end. According to His promise, Jesus Christ will return personally and visibly in glory to the earth; the dead will be raised; and Christ will judge all men in righteousness. The unrighteous will be consigned to Hell, the place of everlasting punishment. The righteous in their resurrected and glorified bodies will receive their reward and will dwell forever in Heaven with the Lord.

Isaiah2:4; 11:9; Matthew 16:27; 18:8-9; 19:28; 24:27 ,30 ,36,44; 25:31-46; 26:64; Mark 8:38; 9:43-48; Luke 12:40, 48; 16:19-26; 17:22-37; 21:27-28; John 14:1-3; Acts 1:11; 17:31; Romans 14:10.

XI EVANGLEISM AND MISSIONS

It is the duty and privilege of every follower of Christ and of every church of the Lord Jesus Christ to endeavor to make disciples of all nations. The new birth of man's spirit by God's Holy Spirit means the birth of love for others. Missionary efforts on the part of all rests thus upon a spiritual necessity of the regenerate life, and is expressly and repeatedly commanded in the teachings of Christ. The Lord Jesus Christ has commanded the preaching of the gospel to all nations. It is the duty of every child of God to seek constantly to win the lost to Christ by verbal witness under girded by a Christian lifestyle, and by other methods in harmony with the gospel of Christ.

Genesis 12:1-3; Exodus 19:5-6; Isaiah 6:1-8; Matthew 9:37-38; 10:5-15; 13:18-30, 37-43; 16:19; 22:9-10; 24:14; 28:18-20; Luke 10:1-18; 24:46-53; John 14:11-12; 15:7-8,16; 17:15; 20:21; Acts 1:8; 2; 8:26-40; 10:42-48; 13:2-3; Romans 10:13-15; Ephesians 3:1-11; 1 Thessalonians 1:8; 2 Timothy 4:5; Hebrews 2:1-3; 11:39-12:2; 1 Peter 2:4-10; Revelation 22:17.

XII EDUCATION

Christianity is the faith of enlightenment and intelligence. In Jesus Christ abide all the treasures of wisdom and knowledge. All sound learning is, therefore, part of our Christian heritage. The new birth opens all human faculties and creates a thirst for knowledge. Moreover, the cause of education in the Kingdom of Christ is coordinate with the causes of missions and general benevolence, and should receive along with these the liberal support of the churches. An adequate system of Christian education is necessary to a complete spiritual program for Christ's people.

In Christian education there should be a proper balance between academic freedom and academic responsibility. Freedom in any orderly relationship of human life is always limited by the pre-eminence of Jesus Christ, by the distinct purpose for which the school exists.

Deuteronomy 4:1, 5, 9, 14; 6:1-10; 31:12-13; Nehemiah 8:1-8; Job 28:28; Psalms 19:7 ff.; 119:11; Proverbs 3:13ff.; 4:1-10; 8:1-7,11; 15:14; Ecclesiastes 7:19; Matthew 5:2; 7:24 ff; 28:19-20; Luke 2:40; 1 Corinthians 1:18-31; Ephesians 4:11-16; Philippians 4:8; Colossians 2:3,8-9; 1 Timothy 1:3-7; 2 Timothy 2:15; 3:14-17; Hebrews 5:1206; 3; James 1:5; 3

XIII STEWARDSHIP

God is the source of all blessings, temporal and spiritual; all that we have and are we owe to Him. Christians have a spiritual debtorship to the whole world, a holy trusteeship in the gospel, and a binding stewardship in their possessions. They are therefore under obligation to serve Him with their time, talents, and material possessions; and should recognize all these as entrusted to them to use for the glory of God and for helping others. According to the Scriptures, Christians should contribute of their means cheerfully, regularly, systemically, proportionately, and liberally for the advancement of the Redeemer's cause on earth.

Genesis 14:20; Leviticus 27:30-32; Deuteronomy 8:18; Malachi 3:8-12; Matthew 6:1-4, 19-21; 23:23; 25:14-29; Luke 12:16-21, 42; 16:1-13; Acts 2:44-47; 5:1-11; 17:24-25; 20:35; Romans 6:6-22; 12:1-2; 1 Corinthians 4:1-2; 6:19-20; 12; 16:1-4, 2 Corinthians 8-9; 12:15; Philippians 4:10-19; 1 Peter 1:18-19.

XIV COOPERATION

Christ's people should, as occasion requires, organize such associations and conventions as may best secure cooperation for the great objects of the Kingdom of God. Such organizations have no authority over one another in the churches. They are voluntary and advisory bodies designed to elicit, combine, and direct the energies of our people in the most effective manner. Members of the New Testament churches should cooperate with one another in carrying forward the missionary, educational, and benevolent ministries for the extension of the Christ's Kingdom. Christian unity in the New Testament sense is spiritual harmony and voluntary cooperation for common ends by various groups of Christ's people. Cooperation is desirable between the various Christian denominations, when the end to be attained is itself justified, and when such cooperation involves no violation of conscience or compromise of loyalty to Christ and His Word as revealed in the New Testament.

Exodus 17:12; 18:17ff; Judges 7:21; Ezra 1:3-4; 2:68-69; 5:14-15; Nehemiah 4; 8:1-5; Matthew 10:5-15; 20:1-16; 22:1-10; 28:19-20; Mark 2:3; Luke 10:1ff; Acts 1:13-14; 2:1ff.; 4:31-37; 13:2-3; 15:1-35; 1 Corinthians 1:10-17; 3:5-15; 12; 2 Corinthians 8-9; Galatians 1:6-10; Ephesians 4:1-16; Philippians 1:15-28.

XV THE CHRISTIAN AND SOCIAL ORDER

All Christians are under obligation to seek to make the will of Christ supreme in our own lives and in human society. Means and methods used for the improvement of society and the establishment of righteousness among men can be truly and permanently helpful only when they are rooted in the regeneration of the individual by the saving grace of God in Jesus Christ. In the spirit of Christ, Christians should oppose to racism, any form of greed, selfishness, and vice, and all forms of sexual immorality, including adultery, homosexuality, and pornography. We should work to provide for the orphaned, the needy, the abused, the aged, the helpless, and the sick. We should speak on behalf of the unborn and contend for the sanctity of all human life from conception to natural death. Every Christian should seek to bring industry, government, and society as a whole under the sway of the principles of righteousness, truth, and brotherly love. In order to promote these ends Christians should be ready to work with all men of good will in any good cause, always be careful to act in the spirit of love without compromising their loyalty to Christ and His truth.

Exodus 20:3-17; Leviticus 6:2-5; Deuteronomy 10:12; 27:17; Psalm 101:5; Micah 6:8; Zechariah 8:16; Matthew 5:13-16, 43-48; 22:36-40; 25:35; Mark 1:29-34; 2:3ff; 10:21 ; Luke 4:18-21; 10:27-37; 20:25; John 15:12; 17:15; Romans 12-14; 1 Corinthians 5:9-10;

6:1-7; 7:20-24; 10:23-11:1; Galatians 3:26-28; Ephesians 6:5-9; Colossians 3:12-17; 1 Thessalonians 3:12; Philemon; James 1:27; 2:8

XVI PEACE AND WAR

It is the duty of Christians to seek peace with all men on principles of righteousness. In accordance with the spirit and teaching of Christ they should do all in their power to put an end to war.

The true remedy for the war spirit is the gospel of our Lord. The supreme need of the world is the acceptance of His teachings in all the affairs of men and nations, and the practical application of His law of love. Christian people throughout the world should pray for the reign of the Prince of Peace.

Isaiah 2:4; Matthew 5:9, 38-48; 6:33; 26:52; Luke 22:36, 38; Romans 12:18-19; 13:1-7; 14:19; Hebrews 12:14; James 4:1-2.

XVII RELIGIOUS LIBERTY

God alone is Lord of the conscience, and He has left it free from the doctrines and commandments of men which are contrary to His Word or not contained in it. Church and state should be separate. The state owes every church protection and full freedom in the pursuit of its spiritual ends. In providing for such freedom no ecclesiastical group or denomination should be favored by the state more than others. Civil government being ordained of God, it is the duty of Christians to render loyal obedience thereto in all things not contrary to the revealed will of God. The church should not resort to the civil power to carry on its work. The spirit of Christ contemplates spiritual means alone for the pursuit of its ends. The state has no right to impose penalties for religious opinions of any kind. The state has no right to impose taxes for the support of any form of religion. A free church in a free state is the Christian ideal, and this implies the right of free and unhindered access to God on the part of all men, and the right to form and propagate opinions in the sphere of religion without interference by the civil power.

Genesis 1:27; 2:7; Matthew 6:6-7, 24; 16:26; 22:21; John 8:36; Acts 4:19-20; Romans 6:1-2; 13:1-7; Galatians 5:1, 13; Philippians 3:20; 1 Timothy 2:1-2; James 4:12; 1 Peter 2:12-17; 3:11-17; 4:12-19.

XVIII THE FAMILY

God has ordained the family as the foundational institution of human society. It is composed of persons related to one another by marriage, blood, or adoption.

Marriage is the uniting of one man and one woman in covenant commitment for a lifetime. It is God's unique gift to reveal a union between Christ and His church and to provide for the man and the woman in marriage the framework for intimate companionship, the channel of sexual expression according to biblical standards, and the means for procreation of the human race.

The husband and wife are of equal worth before God, since both are created in God's image. The marriage relationship models the way God relates to His people. A husband is to love His wife as Christ loved the church. He has the God-given responsibility to provide for, to protect, and to lead his family. A wife is to submit herself graciously to the servant leadership of her husband even as the church willfully submits to the headship of Christ. She, being in the image of God as is her husband and thus equal to him, has the God-given responsibility to respect her husband and to serve as his helper in managing the household and nurturing the next generation.

Children, from the moment of conception, are a blessing and heritage from the Lord. Parents are to demonstrate to their children God's pattern of marriage. Parents are to teach their children spiritual and moral values and to lead them, through consistent lifestyle example and loving discipline, to make choices based on biblical truth. Children are to honor and obey their parents.

Genesis 1:26-28; 2:15; 3:1-20; Exodus 20:12; Deuteronomy 6:4-9; Joshua24:15; 1 Samuel 1:26-28; Psalms 51:5; 78:1-8; 127; 128; 139:13-16; Proverbs 1:8; 5:15-20; 6:20-22; 12:4; 13:24; 14:1; 17:6; 18:22; 22:6,15; 23:13-14; 24:3; 29:15,17; 31:10-31; Ecclesiastes 4:9-12; 9:9; Malachi 2:14-16; Matthew 5:31-32; 18:2-5; 19:3-9; Mark 10:6-12; Romans 1:18-32; 1 Corinthians 7:1-16; Ephesians 5:21-33; 6:1-4; Colossians 3:18-21; 1 Timothy 5:8, 14; 2 Timothy 1:3-5; Titus 2:3-5; Hebrews 13:4; 1 Peter 3:1-7.

Here's the info I promised you at the beginning of this book. If you wish to comment or ask a question, you may –

Email – **pastordougbooks@gmail.com**

Phone – 928 245 1667

Snail mail – P O Box 1128, St. Johns, AZ, 85936

Constructive critique and criticism is always welcome.

OTHER
CHRISTIAN
BOOKS
By
PASTOR DOUG

PUZZLING THEOLOGY

A modern parable of
the Christians growth.
A must read for the thinker.

THE FISHY PROPHET

A Bible study on the book of
Jonah
with an emphasis on the
CALL of the Christian.

Available from
www.amazon.com/author/dougball